# MEDIAEVAL TEMPLES OF THE DAKHAN

# MEDIAEVAL TEMPLES OF THE DAKHAN

HENRY COUSENS

GYAN

*Published by*

Gyan Publishing House
5, Ansari Road
Daryaganj, New Delhi-110002
Phone: 011-47034999, 9811692060
E-mail: books@gyanbooks.com

*Distribution Network*
gyanbooks.com
India, USA, Canada, UK, Australia



ISBN: 978-93-7133-118-0 (PB)

First Published, 1931

2nd Impression 2025

*Printed at:* Gyan Press, Delhi.



**MEDIAEVAL TEMPLES OF THE DAKHAN**
Author: HENRY COUSENS

*ARCHÆOLOGICAL SURVEY OF INDIA, VOLUME XLVIII, IMPERIAL SERIES.*

# MEDIÆVAL TEMPLES OF THE DAKHAN

BY

HENRY COUSENS, M.R.A.S.,

LATE SUPERINTENDENT, ARCHÆOLOGICAL SURVEY OF INDIA, WESTERN CIRCLE.

PUBLISHED BY THE DIRECTOR GENERAL
ARCHAEOLOGICAL SURVEY OF INDIA
JANPATH, NEW DELHI
1998

*Original edition 1931*
*Reprint 1998*



*Price : Rs. 415.00*

PRINTED AT BENGAL OFFSET WORKS, 335, KHAJOOR ROAD, NEW DELHI - 110005

# CONTENTS.

# LIST OF PLATES.

# LIST OF TEXT ILLUSTRATIONS.

# HISTORICAL NOTE.

SINCE the different parts of the country, whose remains are described in this volume, were under various ruling families at different times, who did not succeed one another directly in the government of the country as a whole, as was the case in Northern Gujarat and the Chalukyan dominions, and, as there are few inscriptions and less tradition connecting any of the buildings with them, it will be unnecessary to go into any detail with regard to their history. It will be sufficient for our purpose to mention the rulers of the several districts during the period covered by the buildings that are described.[1]

The earliest dynasty with which we come into contact, when treating of the structural architectural remains of the Dakhan, is that of the Rāshṭrakūṭas whom we find cutting cave-temples at Elurā, not far from the modern town of Aurangābād. At that time, and until their subjugation by the Chālukyas in the second half of the tenth century A.D., they had the Yādavas as their feudatories in the north, who are said to have been, originally, lords of Mathurā and subsequently of Dvārakā; and it is to the patronage of this family, more than to that of the Rāshṭrakūṭās, that we owe most of the old temples now found in the Dakhan. The Rāshṭrakūṭas had ceased to exist as a ruling family more than half a century before the first stone of the temple of Ambarnātha was laid; and the Śilāhāra chiefs of the Konkaṇ, in whose districts it was raised, had already transferred their allegiance to the re-established family of the Western Chālukyas of Kalyānapura.

The governing lords of the branch of the great Śilāhāra family that was settled in the Northern Konkaṇ, were styled *Mahāmaṇḍalēśvaras*, and it is a record of the *Mahāmaṇḍalēśvara* Mummuṇi, or Māmvāṇi, that we have in the temple of Ambarnātha, which tells us he erected the building in A.D. 1060. He was a feudatory of the Chālukya king Someśvara I., and held his court at the sea-girt capital of Purī, which was probably situated in the middle of the island of Sālsette.[2]

The Yādavas were, at this time, confined to the northern part of the Dakhan, and had also transferred their allegiance from the Rāshṭrakūṭas to the Western Chālukyas. When they first came south under Dṛiḍhaprahāra they are said to have established themselves at Chandrādityapura, the modern Chāndor in

---

[1] For a fuller account see the Bombay Gazetteer, Vol. I, Part II.

[2] See Appendix.

the Nāsik district, where he ruled over Seuṇadeśa, the present Khāndesh, the family intermarrying with the Silāhāras of the Northern Koṅkaṇ. Their capital seems to have been afterwards moved to Sindīnagara (Sinnar), further south, which was founded by Seuṇachandra I. under the name of Seuṇapura, about the middle of the 11th century. Some forty years later we hear of Bhillama III. making the impregnable fortress of Devagiri his capital, which continued to be the head-quarters of the family until its capture by the Muḥammadans in A.D. 1312, when its name was changed to Daulatābād.

Fig. 1—The fort of Daulatābād.

There were, again, minor families ruling small districts under the Yādavas, for we learn that the temple of Maheśvara at Pāṭṇa was completed by a chief, Gōvana, of the Nikumbha family, who was governing in that neighbourhood, in A.D. 1153, and that grants were made to it by his successors Sōidēva and Hēmāḍideva, who are mentioned in another inscription at the same place. At Añjanerī is an inscription of A.D. 1142 recording the erection of a temple, which mentions a Seuṇadeva who was, possibly, another small governor under the Yādavas, and related to them.

At the Mānbhāvas' temple at Vāghlī is a long inscription recording the erection of a temple of Śiva, a *sattra* or half of charity, and a well by a prince Gōvinda or Gōvindarāja. It also records certain endowments and gifts to the same by king Seuṇachandra II. in A.D. 1069. The inscription gives a dynasty of petty chiefs who ruled for about four hundred years previously. and who are said to have come from Dvārakā.

# ARCHITECTURAL NOTE.

WITH but few exceptions the ancient Hindu temples of the Dakhan belong, as a class, to the style denominated by Fergusson the Northern or Indo-Aryan, which was practised under the auspices of the various dynasties that ruled over that part of the country which extends from the borders of the Chālukyan and Drāviḍian districts through North Gujarāt, Central India and Rājputāna to the United Provinces and Orissa, during the period from the sixth to the thirteenth or fourteenth centuries A.D.[1] But it is, more particularly, with that branch of it which was fostered by the Yādava rulers of the Dakhan and their feudatories, to which, in many parts, the term "Hemāḍpanti" has been loosely and indiscriminately applied, that we are now interested. For the purposes of this account the term "Dakhan" is taken to embrace all that country between the Kṛishṇā river, on the south, and the Taptī on the north; and from the Koṅkaṇ, on the west, almost up to Haidarābād on the east.[2]

In most parts of the country the building of these old temples is ascribed to a certain Hemāḍpant, just as those of North Gujarāt and the Kanarese districts are placed to the credit of Siddharājā and Jakanāchārya respectively, while those of Khāndesh are frequently assigned to the Gavali Rājās. Who the latter were, if not the early patriarchal rulers of the Yādava family, it is impossible to say. The earlier caves are ascribed to the Pāṇḍavas or Viśvarkarma, and, like the temples, they are said to have been constructed during a single night. Hemāḍpant is sometimes described as a famous physician who, in return for some great cure which he effected, demanded the construction of three hundred temples;[3] but, more correctly, as the famous minister of Rāmchandradēva, the Yādava king of Devagiri, who lived in the second half of the thirteenth century. This Hemaḍpant, or Hemāḍrī, as he is also called, was a man of many parts who, in addition to his administrative duties, found time to compose several literary works; and, having been much attached to religion, he is credited with having erected some three hundred temples. Having been in a position to command the requisite funds for the purpose, it is quite probable that, like the brothers Tejahpāla and Vastupāla of North Gujarāt, in the

[1] *History of Indian and Eastern Architecture*, Revised Edition, 1910, Vol. II, p. 84.

[2] For a more precise definition of the term, and its extent at different periods in the past, see the *Bombay Gazetteer*, Vol. I, Part II, p. 133.

[3] Similar stories are told in other parts of India. Vikramāditya of Ayodhyā is said to have built 360 temples, and Hemachandra, the Jaina minister to Kumārapāla of Gujarāt, to have erected no less than 1,400.

thirteenth century, he caused a good number of temples to be built, and started a revival in temple building which was followed by others. But the earlier and more decorated examples, found in the Dakhan, were, as we shall see, erected long before his time. The true Hemāḍpanti temples are characterized by heaviness inclining to clumsiness, with severely plain exteriors. This absence of outside figure sculpture may be due to the want of sufficient funds, but that could easily have been met by building fewer and building them better. It is, however, more likely that it was due to the advance of the Muḥammadans, who were merciless iconoclasts and who mutilated and destroyed all they found in their path that savoured at all of idolatry. Images displayed upon the outside of temples would only have exasperated them and invited destruction. It was, no doubt, the uncompromising attitude of Islām which, about this time, caused the building of many temples to be temporarily suspended, and which was taken up again in later times, being finished off, or at least made usable, in a very rough and ready manner.

Compared with the great number of temple remains in North Gujarāt, the Central Provinces and the Kanarese country, those in the Dakhan are very few indeed, and this may be accounted for, in some measure, by the fancy there appears to have been for cave cutting, on which money and energy were exhausted, down to the tenth century at least. The Rāshṭrakūṭas were cutting cave temples in the living rock in the Dakhan while the early Chālukyas, their neighbours on the south, were building massive shrines in cut-stone, and in the Central Provinces elaborate temples were being raised in moulded brickwork.

The earlier buildings are now, without exception, very shaky and in a more or less dilapidated state. This is chiefly due to the material used in their construction—the amygdaloidal trap of the country, quarried, as a rule, on the spot. Though a hard tough stone, it is full of flaws and minute cracks which render it very unsuitable for such parts as beams. The style of these buildings being trabeate, necessitating long beams in most cases, which were loaded with enormous masses of material above, the natural result has been that they have generally cracked through the middle. In the temple of Ambarnātha, for example, there is hardly a sound beam left. But, so long as the supports at either end do not give way, and remain vertical, they usually continue to stand, though cracked, until they eventually collapse through the constant grinding action, at the fracture, pulverizing and chipping the surfaces, unless supported by intermediate struts.

A great deal of mischief has been done by people pilfering the material after the buildings had fallen into disuse, but not so much in these stone temples as in the older brick ones in other parts of the country. Brick was more easily handled than stone by the unskilled villager in the building of his hut. "Buildings are always best preserved in places little frequented, and difficult of access: for, when once a country declines from its primitive splendour, the more inhabitants are left, the quicker ruin will be made. Walls supply stones more easily than quarries, and palaces and temples will be demolished to make stables of granite and cottages of porphyry."[1] This is true all over India.

[1] *Rasselas*, Chapter XXXVIII.

The more decorated style of temple building in the Dakhan began to decline soon after the Muḥammadan invasion and eventually died out; the hand of the *salāt* had forgotten its cunning, or his removal to more congenial and remunerative spheres left no one to carry on his work. Under the sultāns of Gujarāt the Hindu *salāts*, or *sutradāras*, were encouraged to practise their craft, with certain necessary restrictions, upon the magnificent mosques and tombs of their conquerors in that province,[1] and there, as may be seen in such buildings as the temple of Hatisingh at Ahmedābād, the descendants of those builders still follow out, to some extent, the traditions and canons of their forefathers. Other states demanded their skill at this time, such as Māndu, Bīdar and Bijāpur, and, in their practice upon Muḥammadan work they, probably, gradually lost their peculiar knowledge as temple builders. Modern temple work in the Dakhan is in a hybrid style partaking, in great measure, of local Muḥammadan feeling, a fair example of which is seen is the accompanying illustration. Fig. No. 2, and the temple of Sundara Nārāyaṇa at Nāsik on plate CXII.

Fig. 2—A modern temple.

The temples of the Dakhan are of no great size, that of Gondeśvara at Sinnar being about the largest now standing. One factor, in limiting the size of a temple, was the length of the shafts of its loftiest pillars. The shaft, or that portion of the pillar between the top of the base and the neck under the capital, was invariably a single block. In their best work the Hindu builders never constructed a shaft of two or more stones, hence the maximum length depended upon the greatest length of stone it was possible, with the means at their disposal, to get out of the quarry. As all parts of a temple are in strict proportion to one another, it follows that the maximum size of a temple was thus limited by the length of the pillar shaft.

As already noticed, the material used in these buildings is, almost exclusively, the Dakhan trap, and the masonry has been put together without mortar or any cementing material whatever. The blocks have been dressed to fit one another upon level beds, their weight, and that of the superincumbant masses keeping them in position. Much, therefore, depended upon a firm foundation,

[1] See *the Muhammadan Architecture of Ahmadābād*, by Dr. J. Burgess, in two parts.

and this was, without doubt, a weak point. Very little was done in the way of excavating for firm foundations, the hard black earth or the solid rock, so often found at the surface, being deemed sufficient. Upon this was laid a bed of great rough boulders from which the walls directly sprang, the lowest course of dressed masonry being roughly hammer-dressed to fit upon the uneven boulders (See Plate LXXV). Consequently, any settlement or yielding of the foundation, as has frequently been the case, has caused the collapse of the walls above. For reasons of economy or lightness, brick has been occasionally used for the towers and superstructure above the cornice, as in the temple at Kokamthān. There is reason to believe brick was in much greater use in early times, as we find it in the old Buddhist *chaitya* at Ter[1] and the other old temples at the same place, where they are provided with wooden door frames and beams which, in brick buildings, were afterwards in stone. The stone walls, which were of variable thickness, and far heavier than would be built at present, were run up in two shells—an outer and inner—the space between being filled in with loose boulders or dry rubble. There is a conspicuous absence of through or bond stones or clamps, and there are many instances where the outer shell has fallen away, leaving the inner intact and supporting the roof, so that a person standing inside the building would not notice anything wrong with it.

With respect to the orientation of temples it was the usual practice to place those dedicated to Śaiva worship to face either east or west; for instance, Ambarnātha and Aundha face the west while Gondeśvara at Sinnar and Maheśvara at Pāṭṇa face the east. Vaishṇava and Jaina shrines may face these points and also the north, temples to Kṛishṇa being generally found facing the latter direction. Temples to goddesses are also found facing the north, while those to Gaṇapati generally face the south.

Although many features are common to both, there is a very marked difference between the style of the early Dakhan temples and the Chālukyan[2] of the same age, and this reveals itself mostly in the *śikhara*, or towers, and the pillars. The Chālukyan style was confined to a much smaller extent of country, and, the land of its origin and development being wedged in between that of the older Drāviḍian of Southern India and the Indo-Aryan of Northern India, it is, as might have been expected, a composite or mixture of both of these, partaking of the characteristics of both. Between the temples of the Dakhan and those of the north there is but little difference, and this is mainly apparent in the towers and pillars. The towers in North Gujarāt,[3] for instance, are clustered *śikharas*, which are made up of a central main tower with smaller ones clustered around and applied to its sides and corners (See Fig. 3). This pattern also pervades Central and Northern India. The Dakhan *śikhara* rises as a single tower, with fretted vertical bands running up each of its four faces. The corners, between the bands, are filled up with horizontal tiers of miniature *śikharas*, diminishing in size to the top, which, in the treatment they have received, have

[1] Archæological Survey of India Annual Report for 1902-03, p. 195.

[2] See *The Chālukyan Architecture of the Kanarese Districts*, by Henry Cousens.

[3] See *The Architectural Antiquities of Northern Gujarāt* by Dr. J. Burgess.

lost their individuality and have become mere decorative detail. There is a third variety of the northern *śikhara* which is made up entirely of vertical

Fig. 3—Types of *śikharas*.

bands, the corners being a repetition of a modified form of *śikhara*, but so disguised as to be hardly noticeable at first sight. This is, perhaps, one of the oldest varieties of the northern type and is found upon seventh and eighth century temples in Orissa, the Bombay Presidency, Central India and as far north as the Kulu valley.

The Dakhan temples occur singly, in groups of individual temples, and in *panchāyatana* groups, that is groups of five shrines—a central main building surrounded by four subsidiary ones arranged symmetrically around it. A complete temple consists of a shrine containing the object of worship, an antechamber before it, a large hall in advance of this again, with either closed in or open sides, and one or more entrance doorways, each with its porch before it. Śaiva temples generally have a small detached pavilion standing out before the main doorway in which was placed a Nandi or Śiva's bull, Vaishṇava temples sometimes have a similar shelter for a *varāha* or boar.

The plans of these buildings are either rectangular in their general outline or star-shaped, and revel in a great multiplicity of angles which are carried up through the walls and the towers; and these, with the numerous horizontal mouldings crossing them, break up the wall surfaces into a bewildering mass of projections and recesses with their sparking lights and deep shadows. A reference to the plans illustrated in the following plates will shew, at a glance, how these are designed. The star-shaped plan is arrived at by revolving a square about its centre—in this case the centre of the shrine or hall—the angles being thus all right angles. There is, therefore, nothing very different between the plans of the Dakhan temples and those of Gujarāt and the north generally. Chālukyan temples have, as a rule, larger pillared halls, and often two—an inner closed one and an outer open hall. There are other variations of plans, such as those with three shrines arranged around the common hall, and others where a number of shrines line each side of the hall, both of which are found at Balsāne.

The walls and wall mouldings differ little from those of North Gujarāt, but more so from those of the Chālukyan temples. There are four marked varieties, namely, (1) the much decorated with sculptured panels filled with an imposing array of deities and other images, such as the Ambarnātha and Balsāne shrines; (2) those equally decorated but with few images, most of the panels being filled with lozenge-shaped ornament, little pillasters or arabesque, as in the temple of Gondeśvara at Sinnar; (3) those decorated mainly with running bands of arabesque as in the temples of Saṅgameśvara, Baleśvara at Pedgāon, Ratanvādi, Devalāna and others; and (4) the latest with plain heavy exteriors and little or no attempt at decoration —the Hemaḍpanti class—like those at Limpangāon and Karjat.

As the Dakhan temples are found spread over that part of the country in which the bulk of the older cave-temples occurs it would be natural to expect to see some analogy between the architectural details of both, but it is surprising to find how little there is. A greater likeness is found between the cave work and that of the seventh and eighth century temples of the early Chālukyas. In the first place, the cave-temples, beyond a small amount of ornamental façade, have no exteriors, and the principal features of the interiors, that we can compare with the later work, are the pillars, doors and decorative detail.

In the pillars we find little in common so far as their general outlines are concerned; but, in their details, the cave pillars present some earlier forms. The characteristic pot and the cushion capitals, and the pot bases of the earlier caves, such as at Kārli and Elephanta, are not found in those early forms in the structural temple work, but those of the later can, in some cases, be traced back to the earlier forms. The pot and foliage feature which, in the cave-temples and in its more stereotyped form in Gujarāt and the Dakhan, is so universally used, does not occur upon the pillars of Chālukyan temples, but it is found as a very conspicuous ornament alone upon the walls of porches and in similar positions. Figure 118 in Fergusson's *History of Indian and Eastern Architecture* (Volume I, Revised Ed.) shows this in its simplest and most natural form as it occurs upon a pillar in cave XIX at Ajantā, and it may be compared with the same feature upon the pillars in the Tringalvādi cave (Fig. 10) and the temple of Lakshmī-Nārāyaṇa at Pedgāon (Plate LXXXIII).[1] Above the pot and foliage in the first is seen the *kīrtimukha* face which is so much used in the ornamental detail of both the caves and the later temples. This is noticed more fully further on.

[1] See the remarks upon the pot and foliage member in *The History of Indian and Eastern Architecture*, Vol. I, p. 300.

The prevailing type of pillar used in the Dakhan is that which is found in the Pāṭṇa temple (Plate XXX), but there are numerous varieties as will be seen in the plates which follow. They differ considerably from those of North Gujarāt, and still more from those of the Chālukyan temples to the south. On the brackets, under the beams above the capitals, are found the little fat *kichaka* figures, a kind of squat Atlantes (see Fig. 11), and sometimes rolled brackets with a cobra head upon the rolls. The former do not occur upon the cave or Chālukyan pillars, but they do on those in Gujarāt. A handsome type of pillar is that in the temple of Lakshmi-Nārāyaṇa at Pedgāon where the pot and foliage occupies a very definite position upon the shaft. In late temples this is replaced by a plain or slightly decorated square block. The style of pillar seen in the temple of Āeśvara at Sinnar, which is scored into a bundle of recessed angles all the way up the shaft, is rare. It may be seen again in the porch before a small shrine near the top of the defile at Lonār lake in Berār. Somewhat like them, though not nearly so much corrugated, are those in the porches of the Ambarnātha temple.

There is less difference in the style of the doorways of the temples, in the three provinces compared, than in any other feature, except, perhaps, the decorated ceilings. Yet no two are exactly alike in their detailed reatment. Over the doors of the Dakhan Śaiva temples Gaṇapati is usually the presiding deity, just as he is in Gujarāt, whereas in the Chālukyan temples it is Gaja-Lakshmī. The Jaina temples have, of course, as elsewhere, a Jina. Gaṇapati has always been a favourite deity in the Dakhan, and he is generally invoked at the beginning of a new year or any new undertaking. New ledgers are opened in his name, and his birthday is kept up with considerable parade, when his images are well to the fore. Being the god of wisdom and Śiva's favourite son, it is appropriate that he should be found in this position. As in Gujarāt the *kīrti-mukha* mask adorns the threshold of the doorway. The proportion of height to width of the door openings is, roughly, two to one, which is a very pleasing proportion; and the width of the vertical mouldings on either side is often about the same as the opening.

Like those of the Northern Gujarāt and Chālukyan temples, the ceilings are a very conspicuous feature in the general scheme of decoration of the interiors. Being almost invisible in the gloom which ever broods over the deity enthroned in the innermost shrine, the ceiling of the sanctum is, as a rule, designed in a very simple manner; but that of the great hall or *sabhamaṇḍapa* is often a veritable work of art. In the older temples these are usually domical in outline, though the domes are not constructed with radiating voussiors as western domes are. A ceiling, in its simplest form, is no more than one or more flat slabs laid across above four beams forming a square, which are supported upon four pillars or four walls. This is the case in ceilings of the smallest span, but, as the span increases, other devices are used to cover in the larger space. Triangular slabs are then laid across the corners of the square formed by the beams, so as to reduce the opening to a smaller square set diagonally to that of the beams, and, if necessary corner slabs are again placed above these, and so on, until the opening is small enough to be closed up by a single square slab. These may then be carved and decorated, a favourite ornamental detail for these simpler ceilings being the rosette or conventional lotus. Such ceilings are generally found in the side bays and corners of the hall.

In the largest class of domical ceilings the distance apart at which the four main pillars are set necessitates the insertion of two intermediate pillars on each side of the square, and these are so placed that their points of support form the corners of an octagon within the square. From this, triangular slabs filling in the corners, the octagon is worked up to a circle which forms the base of the dome. This is constructed of ascending concentric and diminishing rings of stones laid upon horizontal beds, each ring being corbelled forward until they meet at the crown, the keystone, together with one or more of the rings immediately around it, forming a pendant. These rings are kept in position by being locked within the mass of the filling-in of the haunches above. The under sides of these stones, which were, no doubt, roughly dressed before being put in position, were carved into rings of cusped and ribbed mouldings, each little cusp having its own small pendant.

Much of all this fine work is hardly seen owing to the defective lighting of these temples; and, whether this was designedly so or not, it is hard to say. There is no doubt that an added amount of mystery and a feeling of the occult are gained by surrounding an object of worship with a mantle of gloom, the powers of darkness deeply impressing the simple-minded worshipper with the requisite fear and awe upon approaching the sanctuary. Windows are very seldom to be found, and where they have been used they are so filled up with stone grating or perforated arabesque that very little light filters through.

The first thing that strikes one, when examining the image sculpture upon these temples, is the apparent absence of drapery. Its existence is only detected, in most cases, by an odd line here and there crossing the legs at the ankle or the breast. The sculptor was always anxious to display the form, and this would have been excusable, in the case of the female form, if they had been able to delineate the human figure with a tolerable amount of success; but their images are not remarkable for beauty of outline or truthfulness to nature. The limbs are without any indication of muscle, the legs being mere drumsticks. It is true that the Indian does not possess the developed muscle of the European, yet he has enough to be plainly seen in the natural limb of a well-grown healthy individual. The idea of muscular display did not occur to the Indian sculptor even in the portrayal of his heroes and warriors. Their strength and prowess were rather expressed by exaggerated action and size of body compared with surrounding figures; and, in their action, there is much more natural vigour and abandon in the earlier cave images. Female charms were made to centre in great hips and breasts; faces are particularly expressionless. There can be little doubt that women of high caste and good social standing wore less clothing above the waist than they do at present in most parts of India, and this is plainly seen in the wall paintings of the Ajanta Caves, where, beyond jewellery and beads, they are represented with, at most, a very thin diaphanous muslin, only noticed from the pattern of the small spots upon it, which more expressed than hid them. The women who were fully clothed from the neck to the ankles were dancing girls and those of that class, the idea being that, with the better class, there was no shame where there was no sin.

Another marked feature with these *mūrtis*, or images, is the amount of jewellery they are represented as wearing. This, of course, denoted wealth. The ropes of pearls and strings of precious stones are carved with a minuteness and accuracy which demanded endless patience on the part of the sculptor. They are disposed about the figure as necklaces, armlets, waistbands and girdles, earrings, bracelets, and festoons hanging from the girdle. Many an image, indeed, appears to be clothed in nothing else but jewellery.

Figure sculpture embraces the modelling of gods and goddesses, *rakshasas* or demons, kings, queens and their attendants, warriors, *jogis* or religious mendicants, dancing girls and a few animals. Among the last are most frequently found the elephant, lion, tiger, horse, bull and the animal vehicles of the gods. The best modelled of these is the elephant; and, as this came easiest to their hand, sculptors just revelled in its repetitions. The worst executed is the horse, and, consequently, it is not so often found upon the walls of their temples. The lion and tiger are mixed up in very heraldic attitudes, and it is not always easy to say which is which, excepting when the mane is distinctly shown. The camel is not found on temples in the Dakhan, nor elsewhere in early work, but it occurs on thirteenth, fourteenth and fifteenth century work in Gujarāt and Rājputāna. In the earlier temples, down to the eighth century, of which we have no examples in the Dakhan except the cave temples, the human figure was more natural and vigorous in its poses, and there was more diversity in its representations. But by the eleventh century these had become crystallized into stereotyped forms—a set form for each character—and these were monotonously repeated in every building in which they appeared at all. The sculptor's hand was tied, and he was thenceforth allowed little or no liberty of action or originality of design. All the deities, except Sūrya, the Sun-god, who has but two, are represented with four or more arms, and the reason for this exception is that sun-worship was introduced from Persia. This is further confirmed by the fact that he is almost always represented as wearing high Persian boots, being the only deity with his feet covered. It is thus easy to differentiate between gods and men. Some of the Hindu deities are blessed with more than one head, while one, at least, has been accommodated with three legs. To describe all these would require another chapter upon mythology, which would carry us beyond the scope of the present volume. Individual deities will be noticed as they occur in the following descriptions of the temples.

In ornamental detail there is very considerable variety; but, in the earlier temples, as exemplified in the temple of Ambarnātha, there was, perhaps, too much of it crowded over the surfaces of the walls. There were not enough plain surfaces left to act as a foil to the ornament, as there was in the temples of the seventh and eighth centuries. Compare, for instance, the walls of the great temple of Virūpāksha at Paṭṭadakal[1] with those of Ambarnātha, or with that at Halebīd, one of the most profusely decorated temples in India.

---

[1] See *The Chālukyan Architecture of the Kanarese Districts.*

Two most notable objects in ornamental detail are the *makara* and the *kīrtimukha*, and these are of universal occurrence all over India. On the *makara* an article has already been written in the Annual Report of the Archæological Survey of India, for the year 1903-4, in which an attempt has been made to connect the animal with the tapir or rhinoceros. A good example of this conventionalised beast is that given on plate XLVI. It is certainly not intended for the alligator or crocodile to which the term "*maggar*" is now applied. The animal not having a tail to speak of in its natural state, the fertile imagination of some early artist has supplied the deficiency with the most wondrous creation in arabesque and floral whorls.

The *kīrtimukha* occurs alone or in combination with the *makara*. This curious "Face of Fame," or mask, is found repeated as a regular band of moulding round the basement of temples. In Gujarāt it is called by the *salāts*, or native builders, a *garāsamukha*, and the moulding a *garāspatti*. It is found as a prominent detail upon many pillars and at the crowns of little ornamental arched niches upon the walls. It also occurs in the corners of ceiling panels, and on the front of the thresholds of doorways. In most cases it appears to be a grotesque caricature of the human face, but, often, as the face of a conventionalised or heraldic lion.[1] In the earlier examples, the face, though grotesque, is a well formed one; in later work the *motif* seems to have been forgotton and it is often difficult to discover any resemblance to a face at all. Some good examples of the earlier type are found at the caves of Ajantā. The origin of the word *kīrtimukha*, which means "Face of Fame," is given in one of the accounts of

Fig. 4—The *kirtimukha* mask.

the doings of the demon Jalandhara. When he attempted to seduce the wife of Śiva, that god produced a terrible being from his third eye who straightway demanded something to devour. Śiva commanded him to devour himself, which he did, all but his head. Śiva being pleased with this performance, declared that henceforward he should be called Kīrtimukha, and that his head should always adorn the doorways of his temples, where everyone should worship it before entering. On account of the presence of the face on the doorstep, it is usual for worshippers to step *over* and not *upon* the threshold.

Minor ornamental detail is crowded upon the mouldings around door frames, and on pillars and beams, amongst it being some very pretty bands of diaper, scroll and lozenge, and bead ornament. There is also much fretted surface tracery.

[1] The lion, and the separate mask, are seen side by side on the temple of Kēdarēśvara at Balagāmve in Maisur. See *The Chālukyan Architecture of the Kanarese Districts.* Plate CXIV.

# TEMPLES IN THE THĀNA DISTRICT.

## AMBARNĀTHA.

THOUGH not strictly within the confines of the Dakhan it will be well to include a description of the old shrine of Ambarnātha since it is of the same style of work as those above the Ghāts. It is a solitary and superb example, which could neither be conveniently included in an account of the Chālukyan temples of the south of those of Gujarāt on the north. Moreover, it is the earliest dated example of the Dakhan style that we have found.

The little village of Ambarnātha is situated about four miles south-east of Kalyān, and a mile and a half west of the Ambarnātha station on the Great Indian Peninsula Railway, in the Thāṇa District. At a short distance to the east of the village, in a hollow upon the bank of a small stream, stands the venerable pile of weather-stained sculptured stone—the old temple of Ambarnātha. It is practically in disuse at present, a solitary *pujāri* attending once or twice a day to strew a few flowers upon its almost deserted *liṅga*. The general mass of the building has a rather heavy and gloomy look, owing, in great measure, to the truncated condition of its *śikhara*, and the absence of the many crowning finials of the roof which originally lightened its otherwise heavy outline. Upon closer inspection the mass breaks up into a thousand facets of light and shade, and the rich and multitudinous carvings of its surface reveal themselves in all their fantasy of design and form. The walls are found to be cunningly arranged in alternate projections and recesses. These, again, are crossed by horizontal lines of deeply cut mouldings, which, with the great profusion of images, large and small, produce a most bewildering but, withal, pleasing effect of *chiaroscuro*. (Plates III—XI.)

At the back of the temple, the stream is dammed up at this point to form a long deep pool, and, upon its still surface, fringed with reeds and boulders, are reflected the old gnarled branches of the trees that overhang its grassy banks, and the lights and shadows of the fretted temple in the background. The flaming blossoms of the scarlet *palasa* stand out in gorgeous contrast with the purplish-black masonry of the shrine. The temple being in ruins, and well-nigh deserted by human beings, it is a peaceful spot whose quiet is broken only by the busy *mainas* in the trees above or the occasional splash of a solitary kingfisher in the pool. From the walls of the temple rows of sleepy-eyed deities look down complacently upon the comings and goings of the infrequent pilgrim or casual visitor as they have ever done during the long, long centuries, and still they hold their own counsel. Could we but see all their stoney eyes have looked upon through those ages, what a strange panorama of life would unfold itself!

Though the gods without are silent, their lips being sealed, the stones within cry out; and, with no uncertain voice, they tell us something of the origin of this *chef-d'œuvre* of the builder's art. Upon a beam, above the inside of the north door of the hall, is engraved an inscription which records that in *Saka* 982 (A.D. 1060) this temple was built (possibly upon the site of an older one) during the reign of the Śilāhāra chief Mummuṇi or Māmvāṇi. We shall notice it in more detail further on.

The original enclosure around the temple, which has been walled about, measures some fifty yards from east to west by thirty-five from north to south. The temple itself measures 89 feet by 73½ feet. About fifteen yards to the west of the temple are the ruins of two carved gateways. Close to the temple on the south-west is a small tank entered by a carved doorway and surrounded by a ruined wall.

The temple faces the west, and is made up of the sanctum and *maṇḍapa* or hall, the latter being provided with three entrances, each with its own porch. Four free-standing pillars support the ceiling of the hall; and these, with six others in the three porches, are all that are found in the temple. The plan, as will be seen, is peculiar, being apparently made up of two squares set diagonally to one another, touching corner to corner—the smaller being the shrine, the larger the hall. But in reality it is formed of two squares touching side to side, whose sides have been whittled down to narrow panels by the deep recessing of the corners into a line of angles running straight between the diminished sides. This produces very unequal thickness in the masonry, but, at the same time, as will be seen in the photograph, these heavy masses come immediately under the heavier portions of the *śikhara* above. In the hall, the recesses of the doorways tend to equalise the thickness of the walls, the weight of the roof being more equally spread over them. Yet there are places where the masonry seems to be dangerously thin. The projections around the walls form so many buttresses to strengthen them. As with all this class of old work, the masonry is put together without cementing material, the stability of the mass depending upon the weight and level bedding of the blocks composing it. The varied treatment of the square, in designing the plans of these temples, the sides being more or less broken up by projections and recesses, tends to produce somewhat fanciful, yet, nevertheless, pleasing-looking figures.

The floor of the shrine is sunk below the outside ground level, and some eight feet lower than that of the hall. It is approached by a flight of steps, space for which is obtained by sacrificing nearly the whole depth of the usual antechamber, thus bringing the shrine door considerably forward. There seems to be little doubt that the original shrine was on the same level as the hall, but that the fall of the *śikhara* crushed down through its floor and destroyed it. Upon both the north and south walls, at a height of eight feet above the present floor, and on the same level as the hall floor, is a broken ledge of masonry which might well be the remains of the slabs of the upper floor where they were built into the wall. Another broken ledge beneath this on the north wall only, four feet seven inches from the floor, will no doubt be all that is left of the broad shelf which is generally found in these shrines. A temple of the same age as this—that of Sūrya at Mudhera in north Gujarāt—was similarly provided with an upper and a lower shrine, the upper, with its *śikhara*, having been blown up with gunpowder by the Muḥammadans. The modern shrine of Somanātha at Paṭṭan in Kāthiāwād has a lower shrine in which the principal *liṅga* is placed, a duplicate, for every day worship, being placed in the upper shrine. This was so arranged at a time when Muḥammadan aggression was feared, when the entrance to the lower was closed and the iconoclasts were allowed to wreak their vengeance upon the upper or dummy *liṅga*.

The *liṅga* is but a projecting lump of natural rock, and, for that reason, probably, a much more sacred object than the one which was in the upper shrine. A natural rock *liṅga*, like this, is in the shrine of the celebrated *jyotirliṅga* temple of Oṁkāra at Māndhāthā on the Narmadā in the Central Provinces.

**Fig. 5.—Pillar in the temple of Ambarnātha.**

The small shrine on the north-east corner of the hall has been a later addition to the building.

Of the pillars there are three varieties. The four in the hall are alike and are richly carved (Fig. 5). They are somewhat similar in style to those in Vimala Śā's temple at Ābu and the old temple of Somanātha at Paṭṭan. A second variety is found in the main, or west, and the south porches, while those in the north porch differ again from these, though not so much as they all do from those in the hall. The principal difference in the porch pillars is that, while those in the west and south porch rise from the square to round necks and round capitals, those in the north porch continue the square plan all the way up. It might have been expected that, since the side porches are symmetrically placed with reference to the whole building, their pillars would have been of the same pattern, even though those of the main porch differed. The pilasters correspond, more or less, with the pillars which stand before them.

The ceiling panels, within the hall, are very richly decorated in the prevalent style of the best work of the eleventh century. In the central bay, which rests upon the four heavy beams over the four central pillars, is the main dome. It rises in a series of concentric circles to a central pendant. The lowest circle is decorated with a running scroll, while the remaining four are scooped out into half cup-shaped and cusped hollows. These allow of an effective play of light and shade. The triangular spaces in the corners, between the angle of the beams and the edge of the circle, are filled in with the *kīrtimukha* face and scrollwork. Between the central dome and the shrine doorway are two flat ceiling panels which are repeated in the recesses of the three entrance doorways. These are decorated with lotus rosettes and other flat ornament. The ceiling, upon three sides, between the columns and the walls, is coved downwards from the inner square to the walls, and this is decorated with two tiers of ribbing with lozenge-shaped rosettes between the ribs. The ceilings of the porches are flat. In the hall the faces of the beams are decorated with rows of little figures in miniature pillared niches, and a string course of these runs round the tops of the walls just under the coved ceiling. This string course is broken above the north entrance by a curious group of sculpture which will be noticed again in connection with the inscription below it.

The doorways are of the style generally found in these temples, and are adorned with the usual mouldings. A slender pilaster on either side, at the base of which are small standing figures, supports the two ends of the overhanging cornice, each being set in the middle of a group of vigorously cut vertical mouldings. Above the cornice is a row of small figures set in little pillared niches, the central seated figure being Śiva. The raised threshold of the doorway has a *kīrtimukha* face on either side of the central boss; and, before it, is the ornamental *ardhachandra*, or low step, like a half round mat.

A noticeable feature, in the basement mouldings on the exterior, is the torus or half round moulding, immediately under the *garāspaṭṭi* or line of *kīrtimukha* faces. This follows more the section of the moulding as found in very old temples. It will hardly be found again in later work as it changes to a knife-edged moulding, somewhat wedge-shaped in section, as in the temples at Balsāne for example. No temple, unless it be of the largest class, has a complete series of mouldings in the basement, certain of them being omitted, in a regular order, as the dimensions of the building decrease. Here we find three missing, *viz.*, the *chajali* which should come in between the round moulding, described above, and the *garāspaṭṭi* or band of faces; the *aśvathara* or horse moulding which should have come immediately above the band of elephants, and the *narathara*, or band of men, which is usually the topmost moulding of the basement. The top of the basement series of mouldings should always be on the same level as the floor of the hall, and it is so in this case. The band of scrollwork does not belong to the *pīṭha* or basement but to the *maṇḍora* or walls. In the basement of the great temple of Somanātha, at Paṭṭan, these three missing bands are found, the full complement of mouldings being inserted.

The walls proper, or *maṇḍora*, from the basement to the cornice, have the ordinary mouldings and figure panels. In the Somanātha temple, in order to get extra height for the larger structure, the *jangha*, or band of figure panels, is duplicated. It is in this band that the principal images, which adorn a temple, are found. They are made up of gods and goddesses, *yogis* and dancing girls with, now and again, some quaint sculpture thrown in. There are three principal niches on the outside of the walls of the shrine—one in the centre of each—and it is from the images in these that it is possible to determine the deity to whom the temple was dedicated. This especially applies to the niche on the back wall of the shrine. In this case it contains a threefold image, or, at least, an image with three faces, which appears to represent the *trimūrti*, or trinity of the three gods Siva, Brahmā and Vishṇu. It is a standing male figure with three faces and eight arms, but all of the latter are broken off, save the upper left, which holds the serpent of Śiva. The more usual way of representing the *trimūrti* is by a bust only, with three faces, such as we find it in the Elephanta and Elurā caves and in the temples on Chitorgaḍh. On the north side the principal niche is occupied by Mahākālī, one of the forms of Pārvatī, the wife of Śiva, while below her, in the basement niche, is Brahmā with his wife upon his knee. This image had been mistaken for another *trimūrti*, but the fact of the wife being present should dissipate this idea; for, in that case, she would be the common wife of the three divinities! Moreover, the faces are bearded, which is usually the case with Brahmā but not with the *trimūrti*. Then, again, the symbols held in the hands are all those of Brahmā—the *śālunkā* staff, the book, bound round with cord, the rosary and the waterpot. Brahmā's goose, or what remains of it, is seen below his right knee. The central niche on the south side has Śiva dancing the *tāṇḍava* as Naṭeśvara. The basement niche, below this, is empty, as is also that on the east side beneath the *trimūrti*. Above Mahākālī, on the north side, is a mutilated image which appears to be another *trimūrti*, and above this, again, in a circular niche, is Naṭeśvara. A small image of Brahmā is seen up above the *trimūrti* on the east face. The roof, from the cornice upwards, is in what Fergusson designates the Northern or Aryan style, which has been described in the Architectural Note. Quite half the tower has fallen, but it is not difficult to reconstruct it from more complete examples, elsewhere, of the same class. The tower has had rather a fine frontispiece, judging from the fragment that remains of this above the roof of the hall.

The temple has been surrounded by a courtyard containing smaller buildings, but it is now a ruin, and most of the material has disappeared. There was, no doubt, a pavilion right in front of the west or main entrance, under which the Nandi or bull rested, facing the shrine. This has gone and a Nandi, which is probably not the original one, now occupies the main porch. On the south side of the courtyard is a small square tank with steps leading down to the water.

It remains to notice the inscription. This, as already stated, is inscribed upon a beam above, and inside, the north doorway of the hall. It tells us that in *Saka Samvat* 982 (A.D. 1060), during the reign of the illustrious *Mahāmaṇḍaleśvara* Māmvānirājadeva, and while certain ministers of his, who are mentioned by name, were in power, the temple of Śrī Amranātha was built, or rebuilt, (the text is not very clear). Built or rebuilt matters little, for the rebuilding, if there had been any, would simply mean the erection of the present temple, in the place of an older one, which was possibly in brick and thatch. There has been a difference of opinion as to the first figure in the date. It is an unusual form and somewhat like a 7, which some scholars thought it was, while others considered it a 9. The style of the temple, when compared with others elsewhere, is undoubtedly of the 11th century A.D. and certainly not of the 8th, and there is no reason to suppose the inscription refers to an older temple or has been brought from anywhere else. The beam, on which it is, is an integral part of the temple, and fits its place as accurately as any other in the temple. There is not a vestige of sculptured stonework of a 8th century or earlier building; the few sculptured fragments found built into the masonry of the present temple, in other than their proper positions, are nothing more than spoilt and rejected blocks used up as "filling-in." We frequently find the same in other temples. This identical form for 9 has been found on a set of Śilāhāra copper plates, found at Thāṇa by Mr. K. B. Pāthak, in which the date 1049 is expressed in words as well as numerals, thus removing all doubt about it.

The Māmvāṇi or Mummuṇi of the inscription was one of the Śilāhāra *Mahāmaṇḍalēśvaras* of the northern Koṅkaṇ whose capital was Purī, which was possibly situated on Sālsette island near the Kondivte caves, and five or six miles south of those of Kaṇheri, where, in spite of the clearances and appropriations of the Portuguese, and the Muḥammadans before them, there are still a few remains of the Hindu period both above and below ground.[1] The great feudatory family of the Śilāhāras was divided into three main branches, one of which ruled over the Northern Koṅkaṇ while the other two governed the Southern Koṅkaṇ and the districts around Karād and Kolhāpur respectively. The Śilāhāras of the Northern Koṅkaṇ were tributary to the Rashṭrakūṭas and the later Chālukyas of Kalyāna. Māmvāni was thus, in all probability, a feudatory of the Chālukya king Somēśvara I. They carried the *suvarna-Garuḍa-dhvaja*, or the 'Banner of the Golden Garuḍa,' which device is found upon their copper-plate grants. They bore the hereditary title of *Tagarapura-paramēśvara*, or 'Supreme Lord of the city of Tagarapura,' commemorative of their original home. In the Kaṇheri Caves is one of their inscriptions, dated in A.D. 842, giving the name of their capital as Purī, and their territory the whole of the Koṅkaṇ. As this records a grant to the Buddhist community at the mount of Kṛishṇagiri (Kaṇheri) it shews that that sect was still flourishing in the Koṅkaṇ in the ninth century, and was worshipping side by side with their Hindu neighbours.

## PĀROL.

There are, in the Northern Koṅkaṇ, a few other mediæval remains which may be mentioned. At Pārol, a village at the base of the eastern slopes of Tungār hill, and about twelve miles north-east of Bassein, are the remains of at least four old Hindu temples, at none of which worship is now carried on. The two called the temples of the big and little pools—the Mothā and Lahāṇ Tānkyas—stand on the southern and northern banks of a stream which runs down the steep side of Tungār. The Lahān Tānkya temple is about half a mile west of Pārol village; it is levelled to the ground and is now represented

[1] See note on Puri in the Appendix.

by a heap of carved stones. The Big Pool or Mothā Tānkya temple, about half a mile further up, is better preserved. It has an older look about it than the temple of Ambarnātha, and its comparatively plain walls contrast with the profusely decorated ones of that temple. There is very little of it left standing—just the back and portions of the side walls of the shrine. (See Plates XII and XIII.)

Of two in the limits of the village of Majavli, one, not more than a few hundred yards south-west of the village site of Pārol, seems to have been the largest of the group. Its superstructure has gone, and only the plinth and some of the steps remain.

## SOPĀRĀ.

Sopārā, situated about six miles north of Bassein and a mile and a quarter in from the sea face, is one of the oldest sites in western India. It was the Suppāraka or Sūrpāraka of early Buddhist writers, the Sorpāraga, Sopāraya and Sopāraka of the Kārli, Nāsik, Nānāghāt and Kaṇheri cave inscriptions, the Soupara of Ptolemy, the Ouppara of the *Periplus*, and the Subara of the early Arab traveller Ma'sūdī. More interesting still, it has been identified with the Ophir of King Solomon. In 1882 a Buddhist *stupa* was opened up here which yielded

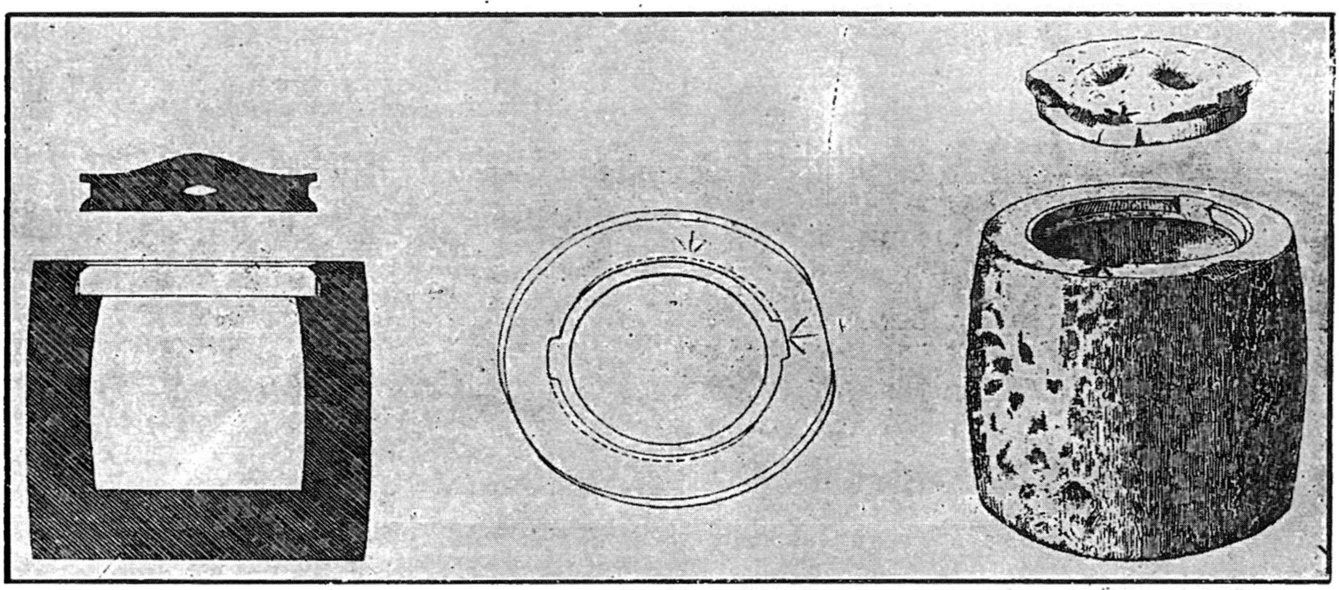

FIG. 6.—Relic box dug up at Sopārā.

very important relics, considered to be nothing less than fragments of Buddha's begging bowl.[1] The base of another *stupa* was subsequently discovered, together with the empty relic casket, which is now in the Museum of the Bombay Branch of the Royal Asiatic Society.[2] Built partly on this mound, its foundations cutting through it, had been a Hindu temple, probably Śaiva, since, among the sculptures scattered about, was a fragment of a huge liṅga. The sculptures lying

[1] For a full account of this most interesting discovery see the late Dr. Bhagvanal Indraji's article in the Journal of the Bombay Branch of the Royal Asiatic Society XV, 273.

[2] See the Progress Report of the Archæological Survey of Western India for the year ending the 30th June 1898.

about around the mound, in an adjacent garden, at the temple on the west bank of the Rāmakuṇḍa, on the east bank of the great Gās *talāv*, and on the west bank of the Nirmal tank were probably intended for this temple which appears to have been left unfinished. The great figure of Brāhmādeva, at the temple on the west bank of the Rāmakuṇḍa,' is an unfinished work, it being left in the rough, and so is one of the images on the bank of the Nirmal tank, which is merely blocked out and is lying where the masons left it. (Plate XIV.)

## BORIVLI.

The oldest remains of a structural building in this part of the country and, perhaps, coeval with the latest cave-temples of Kaṇheri in the neighbourhood, are sundry carved stones of one or more Buddhist temples scattered through the fields between the railway station of Borivli and the caves themselves. The site of one building is on a knoll about a mile east by south from the station. Lying about upon it are some small stone *dāgobas*, whole and in fragments, with remains of brickwork and signs of platforms. These were, probably, votive *dāgobas*, such as are found near the large tank on the top of Chitorgarh in Rājputānā and other Buddhist sites. They are found cut in the rock at the Bhājā caves in one big group. A slight surface clearing on the spot yielded nothing more than a solitary drilled red cornelian bead, like many of those found in such numbers upon the old site of Brāhmanābād in Sind.[1] About a quarter of a mile further on, is a small temple connected with the hamlet of Devī-ka-Pārā, beside which is the site of some Buddhist building or *stūpa*. In the centre was a well-laid brick platform, while, around it, on all four sides, ran one or more walls, of which the traces of foundations and some of the masonry remain. There was not sufficient left from which to form any opinion as to what the building was. A few carved stones lie about with Buddhist symbols upon them, showing that a substantial building of some sort once existed here. The bottom portion of a square stone receptacle was unearthed from the debris,

FIG. 17.—Image of Brāhmā at Sopārā.

[1] Annual Report of the Archæological Survey of India, 1903-4, pl. XLIX.

which had the appearance of part of a relic box similar to the Kolhāpur one in the museum of the Bombay Branch of the Royal Asiatic Society. There are other sites, like the first, hidden away in the jungle in this locality, no doubt once connected with the great Buddhist settlement at the Kaṇheri caves.

At a short distance to the north-west of Borivli railway station, in a field, is a group of seven curious memorial stones, which, on account of their close resemblance to similar stones found in the Kanarese country, have been already described in a previous volume on Chālukyan Architecture.[1] They were probably set up during the time of the Śilāhāras of the Northern Koṅkaṇ; and, judging from the sculptures on them, they commemorated the deaths of heroes who fell in some action carried out upon land and sea. Some of the stones shew the land battle, in which elephants, protected with coats of mail, took part, while others depict the lines of vessels, propelled with banks of oars like the old Roman *biremes*, both in their advance upon the enemy and the melée itself. (Plate XV.)

There is such an action recorded. We are told that the Yādava king, Mahādeva, led his forces against those of the Śilāhāra king of Thāṇa, Somēśvara, and, according to the account of Hemadri, completely subdued him. Mahādeva invaded the Koṅkaṇ with an army consisting of a large number of elephants. Somēśvara was defeated upon land and is said to have then betaken himself to his ships. There somehow he met with his death, probably by drowning, for it is said that even the sea did not protect him, and that he betook himself to the submarine fire, thinking the fire of Mahādēvā's to be more unbearable. The Koṅkaṇ was thereupon annexed by the Yādavas.[2]

## LONĀD.

Five miles to the north of Kalyāṇ, on the other side of the river, is the small and rather insignificant temple of Rāmēśvara at the village of Lonād. It is a Śaiva shrine, but a very plain one compared with that of Ambarnātha. Like the latter, it has a sunken shrine, the floor of which is some three feet below that of the hall. The hall has fallen, and most of its material has been cleared away; but, lying around, are a good many sculptured stones, some of them with very obscene representations. An interesting thing upon one of the basement mouldings of the hall is the name of the ubiquitous *jogi* Magaradhvaja, with the once mysterious number "700" following it. This name occurs upon temples at Mārkaṇḍa, Bilhārī, Amarakaṇṭaka, Chandreha, Khurda, Khajarāha, Chitor in Bihār, in the Khairāgarh state and elsewhere, and the number puzzled the late Sir Alexander Cunningham and his assistants. They looked upon the "700" as indicating a date, but in what era they could not say, since it would fit in with no known era. It is of course impossible for a *jogi*, travelling on foot in the leisurely way they usually do, to have visited all these places in the course

[1] *The Chālukyan Architecture of the Kanarese Districts.*

[2] *Bombay Gazetteer,* Vol. I, Part II. 246.

of one year, so we may at once discard the idea of the number indicating a date. Not long ago a bard when reciting a *kirtāna*, brought in the words, in the middle of it, "Goraknātha and his seven hundred disciples" which at once explained the mysterious number. Magaradhvaja, also, measured his importance by the number of his following: he was the leader of seven hundred disciples.[1]

Sufficient has been said to show that this part of the Koṅkaṇ has been a place of very considerable activity from the beginning of the Christian era down to the times of the Śilāhāra chiefs.

# TEMPLES IN KHĀNDESH.

## BALSĀNE.

THE village of Balsāne is situated upon the north bank of the Burāi stream, at a distance of about twenty-seven miles in a north-westerly direction from Dhulia in Khāndesh. Near the village there are the remains of nine separate old buildings—eight temples and a *maṭha* or monastery. In a field, just above the bank of the stream, to the south-east of the village, are three of them; four are on high ground to the east of the village; the *maṭha* is at a short distance to the north-east of the last group, and there is a small temple in the fields across the river, some distance to the south of the village. Sculptured stones lie about, among which are images of the *panchaliṅga* and Brahmā, and the only inscription is one over the doorway of the *maṭha*. (Plates XVI—XXIV and XXVIII).

Of the temples in the field, first mentioned, two are built parallel and close to one another, both facing west, while the third stands out in front of these and faces east. The larger one of the first two, to the south of the other, has been a very fine triple-shrined building, most elaborately and profusely sculptured, but it is now very shattered and weatherworn. Parts of the *śikharas* of the east, or main, and the south shrines remain, but that of the north has fallen, leaving the walls in a very shaky condition. The temple is of the same style as that of Ambarnātha, though differing in minor details, and the two must have been erected about the same time. It will be seen that the plan is very different, it having three shrines and one porch instead of three porches and one shrine as at Ambarnātha. It faces the west, and has been, from the beginning, a Śaiva temple. The shrine here is not sunk, but is on the same level as the rest of the floor of the building, and the antechamber is of full depth. In the main shrine is a *liṅga* and Nandi, the usual outside pavilion for the latter being absent as at Ambarnātha. The bull here, again, is not the original one. The dedicatory figures over both the shrine and main doorway have been wilfully damaged. The images upon the exterior would point to the south shrine having been occupied by a Vaishṇava deity, but it is now empty. The north shrine is also empty, the images upon its walls, outside, being two *devīs* or goddesses. The east or main shrine held the *liṅga* of Śiva. Over the doors of the two side shrines is Gaṇapati, while, within each, is an altar for an image.

There are six pillars—four in the hall, and two in the porch—of one pattern, and simpler in design than those of Ambarnātha. They have very few images upon them, their place being taken by fretwork designs.

The ceiling patterns are similar to those of Ambarnātha. The central bay is domed, and rises, in two ascending rings of cusped mouldings, to the centre, which then falls in a cusped rosette pendant. The corners, in the angles between the beams and the circle of the dome, are filled with florid *kīrtimukhas*. The marginal ceilings of the hall are coved upwards from the walls to the tops of the beams over the central pillars, and are decorated with lines of ribbing as at Ambarnātha. The ceiling of the shrine is hardly less elaborately decorated than that of the hall, while that in the porch has been like that of the hall, but it is very much weatherworn.

Passing on to the outer walls of the temple, we find them more richly encrusted with ornamental detail and more overlaid with tracery than in the temple of Ambarnātha; in fact, we have here the style in its fullest development, crystallized into its richest details, and sparkling with light and shade from summit to basement. Being a smaller building than Ambarnātha—64 feet over all—the basement is reduced in height by the further omission of the elephant moulding, thus making the basement four mouldings short of the full complement. But there is a change here in the torus moulding of Ambarnātha which has become wedge-shaped with a sharp edge. The walls above the basement are much the same as in that temple except that there is rather more richness in details. The *śikharas*, again, are more lavishly worked. Introduced into the walls will be found a few narrow vertical panels of scrollwork, which, later on, with surface fretwork and lozenge-shaped oranament, were used more fully to take the place of the more expensive image carving, as may be seen on the Kokamthān temple, Gondeśvara at Sinnar, and the temple of Mahādeva at Pāṭṇa. It is, here, but sparingly used.

The principal images on the exterior of the temple are as follows: On the west face of the south shrine the image is much corroded and is not very distinct. On the south face is Narasiṁha, and on the east Trivikrama or the "Three Strides of Vishṇu." On the south face of the main, or east shrine, is Bhairava; on the east Śiva dancing the *tandava*, and on the north face Mahākālī. On the west face of the north shrine is Mahiśāsura-mardanī; on the north is a *devī* (Pārvatī ?) with ten arms, who arranges the ornaments in her hair with two of her right hands, and holds up a mirror in one of her left. Two other hands, one on each side, seem to be tying something about her left leg which is raised towards them—perhaps putting on an anklet. The other niche of this shrine has fallen away. There are the usual indecent figures on the temple, but they are confined to the smaller images on the bands.

Of the same style and age is the decorated temple with the three porches in the group on the east of the village. Here we have a temple on the same general plan as that of Ambarnātha except that, in the plan of the shrine the corners are at different angles with one another. The plan is of the star-shaped variety, as will be found repeated in the temple of Mudhai Devī at Vāghlī and in Gulteśvara at Sarnaī in the Kaira District and elsewhere. The temple faces east. The shrine is a total wreck, sufficient of the basement remaining to show what its plan was like. The ceiling panels, within the hall, are similar to those in the first temple described, save that the marginal coved ceilings, being much broader, struts rise at an angle, from the capitals of the four central pillars, to help to carry the additional weight. In the basement the *garāspatti*, or band of *kīrtimukhas*, is here replaced by a band of rosettes and lozenge-shaped flowers, the former being not unlike the heraldic rose. The shrine doorway, which still stands, is almost identical in design with that of the first temple, and, upon its dedicatory block is Gaṇapatī. Curiously, the *kīrtimukha* faces are absent from the threshold of the first temple but are inserted upon the face of the slender pilaster on either side.

This building is in a very dilapidated state; the stone of which it is built is of a soft nature, and has weathered in many parts to a state of *murum* which now crumbles away at the least touch. The broken masonry, at the back discloses the secret of the construction of its walls. An outer and an inner shell of block masonry, set up more or less on edge, are filled in between with loose blocks and boulders, without the least attempt at bonding, and with no cement of any kind. In fact, the outer and inner shells just keep the 'filling-in' from rolling out altogether. To prevent confusion in the description of these buildings and in the absence of names, they are numbered. This is No. 4. No. 5 is not far from it.

Temples Nos. 2 and 3 in the first group, close to No. 1, and No. 5, are all of a later type by at least fifty years. They are characterized by less complex plans, and are practically free of figure carving on their exterior. No. 2, on the north of No. 1, though so much plainer in design, has its own merits, and cannot be considered a falling off from the more florid style of Nos. 1 and 4. It is a different style altogether, which seems to have been abruptly introduced, and to have been the type from which the later "Hemāḍpanti" of the fourteenth century may have been derived. Were it not that these temples bear the stamp of twelfth century work, one might almost think that the discontinuance of images upon the outside was due to the approach of the Muḥammadans whom the Hindus soon had reason to dread as uncompromising iconoclasts and the most bitter foes of idolatry. Images, out of sight within a temple, might pass unnoticed, but those paraded upon the outside walls would but exasperate them and be a direct invitation to sacrilege.

This particular temple had, like No. 4, a star-shaped plan, though little now is left of it. In its upturned floor—in all probability the work of Muḥammadans in search of treasure—is a huge *liṅga*, while in a large niche in the back wall is a standing female image, the bust alone remaining, the rest having disintegrated away. This was probably an image of Pārvatī in one of her forms; and this being such a prominent and important image, here, it is possible she also occupied the north shrine in temple No. 1.

The roof of the hall has fallen in, the pillars and beams remaining in their places. The type of pillar has changed entirely from those in the hall at Ambarnātha, but those in the north and west porches in the latter temple, stand about midway between the two. They are conspicuous by the absence of figure carving upon them, its place being taken by scroll and fretwork patterns. It will be seen that the pillars of both temples are made up of practically the same parts. The figure panels on the bases of the earlier ones are replaced by triangular facets, and the images upon the lower square part of the shaft are omitted, leaving the surface quite plain. The two bands of sculpture above this are replaced by fretwork panels, the *kīrtimukha* band above this, again, is retained, and so are the triangular ornaments above them. The capital is almost identical, and the whole is surmounted, in each case, by brackets, with squat supporting figures beneath them. There are a few small indecent figures on the walls of this shrine.

Temple No. 3, opposite the last, is, even, a greater wreck. It is of precisely the same style. From the fallen blocks it is seen that it possessed a very finely designed ceiling panel—a small central dome adorned with cusped ornament and florid *kīrtimukha* corners. Gaṇapati presides over the shrine door. The two temples face one another and are built upon the same centre line. This one faces the east. The outside walls are rather plainer than those of No. 2. Around about, in this same field, are what appear to be the sites of other buildings.

Returning to the group on the east of the village we find temple No. 5 a very differently planned one to those we have been considering. There is nothing new to note with reference to the main shrine, and the ceiling of the hall is supported, like others, upon four central pillars. But around the sides of the hall are a series of ten small shrines, as may be seen on the plan. In front of the hall doorway is a verandah-porch with a shrine at each end. As the temple faces the north it could not possibly have been dedicated to Śaiva worship. It was very likely Vaishṇava, the main shrine containing an image of Vishṇu and the ten smaller ones, round the hall, the ten *avatāras* of that deity. Within the main shrine is the image of a horseman, which may possibly be one of these, *viz.*, the *Kalka avatāra*, but at our visit the front of the temple had been walled up, all but a small doorway, and the interior was so dark and filled with the overwhelming strench of bats, that it was not possible then to examine it thoroughly. The pillars and the exterior walls agree in style with those in temple No. 2. Beside the temple, on the same platform, is a little shrine with a partly mutilated standing *devī* somewhat similar to that in the shrine of No. 2. This building is plain and consists of a small shrine and an open antechamber, and it also faces the north. To the west of these is a small, simply constructed temple, very plain, facing east.

Upon a knoll, about a hundred and fifty yards to the north-east of this group, is a low square plain building which is, as an inscription over the doorway declares, a *maṭha* or residence for priests. It consists of a large square room with plain walls, and four central pillars supporting the roof. A doorway leads out into a verandah, now partly destroyed, in each end of which is a small cell-shrine. The doorway has been, unlike those of the temples, fitted with a wooden door, sockets being provided in the stone frame, above and below, for the door to swing in, and large square deep channels in either side, about half way up, for a beam to slide in, behind the door. The outside walls are perfectly plain, and no ornament whatever appears to have been applied.

The inscription which is above the doorway, in five long lines, records the rebuilding of the *matha*, which had been ruined, by Pandita Śrī Mahālūka on the banks of the Kesara at Balasāṇa in Saka 1106 (A.D. 1184). The river is now known as the Burāī.

In addition to the remains already described, there are a small temple about half a mile to the south of the village, several *sati* and memorial stones, and mutilated sculptures in and around the village. One of the best of the memorial stones stands in front of temple No. 5. They are generally tall, square columns—not flat slabs as found in the Kanarese districts—sculptured upon all four faces with representations of warriors, death scenes of the heroes commemorated, their arrival in paradise, the *liṅga* as their object of worship, and other scenes. A group of these stands upon high ground between the river and the village. Amongst other sculptures lying about is a large boar covered with little figures in rows along his back. This may have been connected with the Vaishṇava temple No. 5.

## PĀṬṆĀ.

Pāṭṇā, ten miles to the south-west of Chālisgaon in Khāndesh, is the site of a deserted town, now overgrown with jungle, where, scattered among the ruins, are the remains of several old temples. The range of the Sātmāla hills, running east and west and separating Khāndesh from the Nizām's territory, is at this point recessed, forming a horse-shoe-shaped valley. The hills at the entrance of the valley are about a mile apart, while the glen between them runs back about a mile and a half. At the upper end of the valley, above the temple of Āi Bhavānī on the eastern side, a rough mountain path winds up the lonely ravine—the Pitalkhorā or "Brazen Glen"—at the top of which, in the wild solitude of the rocks, is a group of very old Buddhist caves. A stream, fed by the innumerable rivulets that trickle down the sides of the hills around, winds down the Pāṭṇā valley, in one of its curves sweeping by the shrine of Āi Bhavānī, where there is still kept up a yearly *jatrā* or fair. The stream inclines, throughout its meanderings, towards the eastern side of the valley leaving a considerable area between it and the western cliffs, in which, high up above, are the cave-temples known as Nāgārjuna's Kotri, Sitā's Nhāni, and the Śrinagar Chāuri, a space ample enough for the old town of Pāṭṇā, whose ruins now occupy the ground. The whole of the valley is thickly wooded, and, being quite uninhabited, save by the owl and the jackal, the pig and the panther with an occasional tiger, it is, between the lights, quite an eerie and lonely place to camp in. The ruins of the old town are thickly scattered about, and, with difficulty, maintain their ground against the jungle which, where unable to displace them, just grows over and casts its creeper entanglements firmly around their mouldering walls. (Plates XXV—XXXII.)

Beyond the few ruined temples, tanks and wells, there is now little above ground to represent the more ancient city. The ruins that now exist, composed of mud and rubble stone walls and Musalmān graves, are of a comparatively recent town, and that of no great size. It appears to have been walled in with high mud walls and lofty bastions, as was usual in the Dakhan, within which was a citadel similarly fortified. The crumbling walls of these enclosures, with the foundations of mud and rubble-built houses, still exist. One of the walls runs along east and west by the side of the principal temple, that of Maheśvara, and is built on to it on either side; this makes the temple itself, which is upon high ground, part of the wall, the north face being within, while the south face is without the fort. Opposite this, on the south, and separated from it by a broad passage, is another small fortified enclosure in which is a small ruined temple with an inscription over its doorway. Besides these, there are two other small ruined shrines, which, like them, have been included within the fort wall on its east side. These are a few hundred yards to the east and north-east, respectively, of the first temple, one being Brahmanical and the other Jaina. With the temple of Āi Bhavānī, up the valley, these are all the remains visible of the more ancient city of Pāṭṇā.

The temple of Maheśvara, the largest and most important, is built upon the usual plan with shrine, *maṇḍapa* or hall, and porch. The hall has been an open one, the marginal pillars, supporting the eaves, standing upon a dwarf wall which encloses the hall. There has been but one entrance, on the east side, the direction in which the temple faces. The plan of the shrine is star-shaped, being formed on the basis of a circular star of twenty-eight angles or points. Two points are absorbed, on the north, west and south, in forming the central panels on those sides, and eight have had to make way for the antechamber and entrance. The inside of the shrine is, of course, square. The pillars are of a somewhat later type than those at Ambarnātha or Balsāne, but their design is dignified and their proportions good. The *kīrtimukha* mask, which does not appear in the basement mouldings outside, is used very much as a decorative detail on the pillars, which have absolutely no images upon them.

The shrine doorway, which is neatly decorated, has Gaṇapati upon the dedicatory block above, and on the threshold, on either side of the centre, is the *kīrtimukha*. In a frieze of small niches at the top, above the cornice, are images of Śiva in the centre with the *saptamātṛīs*, or seven mothers, and Gaṇapati on either side of him. In the middle of the floor of the shrine is a *liṅga*, and in the centre of the back wall is a niche to hold an image.

The exterior walls of the temple, though fully decorated, are not so thickly overlaid as those at Balsāne; and what is very noticeable is the absence of much figure sculpture. The only large images have been those in the three principal niches round the shrine and on the central angle of the walls between them. Beneath them, and just above the basement, are small niches with tiny images in them. Beyond these there are no others. The image in the north niche is Mahākālī, and in the south one Bhairava; the west or back niche is empty. The *śikhara*, or spire, has disappeared. There are several images lying about which were probably in some of the niches of the temple, among which are Śiva, Pārvatī, Lakshmī-Narāyaṇa and Sūrya.

Built into the wall of the antechamber, on the south side, is a large inscribed slab, bearing a record in ancient Devanāgarī. It belongs to a chieftain of

Khandesa named Govana, and ancestor of the rulers of 1,600 villages, Sōidēva and Hēmāḍidēva, mentioned in the inscription at the temple of Āi Bhavānī. It records the consecration of a temple of Śiva, which had been begun by Indrarāja, the father of Govana, and had been finished after his death, as well as a grant of a village, called Devasaṁgana, made by Govana on that occasion. Govana's minister was Chāngadeva.[1]

The building beside this one on the south, in the other enclosure, which is now in ruins, seems to have belonged to the larger temple. Its axis, passing through the entrance doorway and the doorway of its enclosure, passes through the centre of the shrine of the large temple ; and it faces the large temple. Its interior is much like the interior of the hall on the south side of the enclosure of the temple of Gondeśvara at Sinnar. It has no shrine, the interior being a long plain hall. It was probably a *maṭha* or resthouse attached to the large temple. Over its entrance doorway, as already mentioned, is a much worn and damaged inscription, just as occurs over the door of the *maṭha* at Balsāne.

Straight in front of the large temple, at a short distance from it, is the small ruined Brahmanical shrine, already mentioned, facing the north ; and, in front of this, about a hundred yards away, is another ruined shrine originally dedicated to a Jina, having a seated Jina over the entrance doorway, and an empty throne seat, well-carved, within the shrine.

At the upper end of the valley, on the east side of the stream, is the old, but very insignificant, temple of Āi Bhavānī. Very little of the original building remains intact, most of what is seen being rebuilt from the material of an older temple. From what little does remain the temple would appear to have been a cluster of small shrines, with one or two small halls. At present the place is in a very ruinous and dirty condition. Built into the outside of the enclosing wall is a much abraided inscription slab, but as this wall has been built partly of old temple materials, this may not be in its original position. The greater part of it is in Sanskrit, the remainder in a kind of old Marāṭhī. Its main object is to record that the chief astrologer of the Yādava king Siṁghaṇa, Changdeva by name, grandson of the well-known astronomer Bhāskarāchārya, founded a college for the study of the *Siddhāntaśiromaṇi* and other works of his grandfather and relations. The college was endowed with land and other sources of income by the brothers Sōidēva and Hēmāḍidēva, two members of the Nikumbha family, who, as feudatories of the Yādavas, ruled over the country of the 1,600 villages. The metrical part of the inscription is followed by a prose passage which records a grant made by Sōidēva in favour of Chāngdēva's college in *Saka* 1128 (A.D. 1206). This grant must, of course, have been made some time before the inscription itself was composed ; for we know, from the preceding, that the inscription was put up during the reign of Siṁghaṇa who began to rule in *Saka* 1131, and at a time when the feudatory Sōidēva was dead and had been succeeded by his younger brother. The inscription itself is not dated, but it may have been composed in the first quarter of the thirteenth century, some time after A.D. 1209-10.[2]

---

[1] *Indian Antiquary*, VIII, 39.
[2] *Epigraphia Indica*, I, 338.

## VĀGHLĪ.

About seven miles to the north-east of Chālisgāon is the village of Vāghlī, where there are the temples of Mudhāidevī, a mile to the south-west of the village, and of Krishṇa in the village. (Plates XXXIII—XXXVI.)

The temple of Mudhāidevī is placed upon an artificial mound upon the bank of the river and is now partly in ruins. Smaller shrines which surrounded it, and stood upon the margins of the platform, have disappeared, save the ruins of one which stood on the south side of the temple. The foundation of a forward porch or *chhatri* are seen at the east end of the platform in line with, and facing, the entrance of the temple, which is turned towards the east. Midway, between the two, a few stones mark the site of a small *kuṇḍa* (tank) or pavilion. The *śikhara* has disappeared.

The temple would seem to have been originally dedicated to Sūrya. Of the three images in the three principal niches around the outside of the shrine walls, that in the back or west niche—the most important one of the three, and always indicating the deity to whom the temple is dedicated—is Sūrya with his seven horses beneath him. That on the north is Mahākālī, and that on the south is Gaṇapati. Lying within the temple are two large corner blocks of what seems to be part of the *vedi* (dwarf parapet wall) of a pavilion or the hall, while, without, is another similar one, on each of which are three well-carved standing images of Sūrya, these being the only images upon them, each of which is about a foot high. On the block above the shrine door is Gaṇapati, who is as universal in the Dakhan, in this position, as Gaja-Lakshmī is in the Kanarese districts. Immediately above it, on another block, is a seated figure which may possibly be that of Sūrya, but it is much corroded and bedaubed. It sits upon a seat, with legs hanging in western fashion, arms depending to the elbows, and the hands brought to the lap, from each of which starts upwards, to either side of the head, what might easily be taken for the stems of Sūrya's lotuses.

In addition to these evidences of the temple having been dedicated to Sūrya there are, in the shrine, door-posts of small shrine doorways, or, perhaps, the flanking posts of the back of a throne, upon one of which Sūrya, in a standing position, is repeated all the way up in little niches.

The exterior of the *maṇḍapa* walls are finished off quite plainly. From this fact it might be inferred that there was an outer corridor with sloping cornice and *vedi* around it, for such a plain flat wall would hardly have been left on the outside of a temple whose shrine walls have been carefully decorated and wrought.

As in the case of the temple of Maheśvara at Pāṭṇā, the shrine of this one has been built on the star-shaped plan of twenty-eight points, two being absorbed in each of the panels on the north, west and south faces, and eight in the antechamber and entrance.

The roof of the hall is supported, within, upon four very plainly decorated pillars, which have no images upon them. The central ceiling, and that of the porch, are square in plan, and rise as hollow truncated pyramids, the sides being decorated with a series of horizontal concave mouldings. From the top hang five rosette pendants. The antechamber is similar, except that it has but one central rosette. The shrine ceiling is circular in plan, rising in diminishing circles of plain mouldings.

Within the shrine, placed upon a temporary altar, is now an image of Śiva-Pārvatī, having Nandi below them. This is all bedaubed with red pigment and is the object worshipped.

The small shrine which stood on the south side of the temple has fallen down bodily over the edge of the platform, which is much broken away here.

The temple of Krishṇa, as it now stands, is of little interest save for three large inscription slabs built into the inner wall of the hall. There is no separate shrine, and what little of the original temple remains has been so encased in mud walls that not even its plan can be made out. One of its ceilings is sculptured in bold relief with a group representing Krishṇa and the *gopis*. Within the hall, upon a raised platform, is an arrangement made up with a brass mask and which is now worshipped as Krishṇa by members of the Mānbhāva sect.

The inscription records the foundation of a *sattra* or hall of charity for travellers and the learned and indigent, and the erection of a temple of Śiva, under the name of Siddheśanātha or Siddheśvara, with a tank or well attached to it, by a prince Govinda or Govindarāja and his wife. The second part of the inscription records various donations in favour of the temple and the charitable institute, made both by Govinda himself and by (his sovereign lord) the *Mahāmaṇḍalanātha*, the illustrious king Seuṇa. The grant was made on the occasion of a solar eclipse which corresponds to Tuesday, 21st July, A.D. 1069. The king Seuṇa is the Devagiri Yādava Seuṇachandra II. A long list of petty ruling chiefs is given, who are said to have come from Dwāraka.[1]

## SANGAMEŚVARA.

About fifteen miles to the north-east of Chālisgāon is the small village of Sangameśvara where, near the junction of the two streams, perched upon the high bank, is the old temple of Mahādeva. It is built upon a very high knoll which was once a stone platform, with, apparently, a brick core. It faces the east, and now consists of the usual shrine, a hall whose roof has disappeared, and a very prolonged porch. The exterior of the temple is perfectly devoid of figure sculpture, its place on the walls being taken by three running bands of geometric ornament. These are exceedingly chaste and effective, and are carried round the three sides of the exterior walls of the hall and shrine in unbroken lines. The long approach to the hall from the porch seems to have been flanked the whole way, on either side, with a dwarf wall and inside bench. The hall is very plain within, there being no free-standing pillars in the middle of the floor. The whole space was covered by a large dome which has fallen, leaving but one ring of its mouldings, which rests upon a polygon of sixteen equal sides. Upon either side of the hall are plain recesses, without doorways or any indications to show that they had been used as shrines. The pillars are, as a

[1] *Epigraphia Indica*, II 21.

rule, plain, but two at the entrance of the porch, and the pilasters, have been decorated with similar surface ornament to that on the bands round the exterior of the temple. (Plates XXVI, XXXIV, XXXVI and XXXVII.)

The ceiling of the antechamber is peculiar, inasmuch as it is oval in design, a very rare form. The rosette in the middle, which forms the pendant, is also oval.

The doorway of the shrine is well sculptured after the style of that of Gondeśvara at Sinnar and Maheśvara at Pāṭṇa, but more squat and clumsy in execution. Over the door, upon the block, is Gaṇeśa, and within the shrine is a *liṅga*. Lying within the hall are several loose images, among which are Gaṇeśa, Mahākālī and Śiva-Pārvatī.

Standing out before the temple is a small modern shrine to Hanumān, and in a row to the south of the temple, and round about its porch, are a number of little *samād* shrines. Lying out before the porch is the mutilated body of a small stone elephant having, on its back, four heads joined together as in the images of Brahmā, and around its back, like the boar at Balsāne, are four rows of seated *devīs*, with some ornamental work, surmounted by the *kīrtimukha* over the tail.

The *śikhara* of the temple has gone.

## CHĀNGDEVA.

Of about the same age as the temple at Sangameśvara is that of Chāṇgdeva at the village of the same name near the junction of the Purnā with the Taptī, fifteen miles east of Bhusāval. It has been a large and fine building, but whether it was ever originally finished or not is not very clear. It has been finished off in later times, with brick and mortar in a very clumsy manner. The whole length of the temple measures 97 feet, and it faces the east. At the entrance there are some inscriptions, but they are much effaced. The roof of the hall has gone, together with some of the pillars, and portions, only, of the lower parts of the walls of the hall remain, upon which mud and brick continuations have been carried up to supply the missing portions. The basement is silted up, and two or three feet of the lower mouldings are buried. The original stone walls end with the string course above the cornice, and it is possible that the *śikhara* was built, or was intended to be built, in brick and plaster as in the temple at Kokamthān in the Ahmednagar District. The temple appears to have been dedicated to Vaishṇava worship. (Plates XXXVIII—XL.)

Upon the broad sculptured band around the shrine walls are some boldly cut images, which stand out in relief from the walls, and are not placed in niches as in the earlier temples. Most of these are female images, the only male ones occupying the principal panels, one on each. On the north, west, and south central panels is a group of three figures, being in each case a male with a female on either side of him, which may well represent Krishṇa and some of his lady friends in whose company he is generally shewn. These male figures are possessed of but two arms each, which show that they cannot claim a higher status than demi-gods or *avatāras*.

As in the temple of Mahādeva at Sangameśvara there is a small oval dome in the antechamber to the shrine. Within the shrine is an image which is said to be that of Chāngdeva. Where the water of ablution runs out through the shrine wall on the north side, there is a very ornamental gargoyle in the shape of a *makara*, much like the one at the temple of Gondeśvara at Sinnar in the Nāsik District.

In the river bed is a temple of modern construction, built, it is said, by Queen Ahalyabāi of Indor, which has come to grief in a curious manner. The whole of the upper part of the temple has tumbled over into the bed of the river *en bloc*, and now lies partly buried in the sand, leaving the lofty platform, upon which it was built, with nothing upon it except the lower courses of the temple plinth. The two styles of construction—the older and the more recent—are well exemplified by these two temples. In the older no mortar was used, the massive blocks

FIG. 8—Temple in the bed of the river at Chāngdeva.

being kept in their places by their own weight, superimposed one upon the other without any cementing material, and, sometimes, with a very sparing use of clamps. It thus naturally follows that when the foundations of such buildings give way the superstructure comes down like a house of cards, the blocks sliding off one another. In the more modern, mortar has been used with smaller blocks; and, the mortar being exceptionally strong, the whole has hardened into a solid mass. The temple of Ahalyabāi having been thus built, went over during a severe flood, in one mass intact. In the bed of the stream at Patunde between Chālisgāon and Vāghlī, is another instance of the great tenacity of mortar in similar circumstances. It is the great square room of what appears to have been a Musalmān mausoleum, canted over off its basement into the sand at such an angle that a person may stand upon the accumulated sand outside and look down into the interior over the tops of the four walls, the dome having slid off. The four walls just hold together in an apparently uninjured state.

## ERANDOL.

In the middle of the town at Erandol, thirty-seven miles east of Dhulia, is a large solidly-built old quadrangle known as the Pāndāva's Vādā. It is the remains of one of those strongly built and enclosed mosques—or rather partly mosque and partly fort—which were erected in the early days of Muḥammadan rule, and is of the general plan upon which the great 'Adina *Masjid* at Anhilvād-Paṭṭan was probably built. Like the latter, the greater part of this building, at the west end of the courtyard, seems to have been built of the remains of older Hindu temples. The courtyard and the mosque were enclosed by a lofty substantial stone wall, having high arched recesses all around the inner side, in each of which is a barred or grated window. There appears to have been a fine porch before the entrance to the courtyard on the east, but it is now represented by a huge pile of fallen masonry, over which the visitor has to climb to reach the interior. The mosque which, as usual. occupied the whole width of the west end of the enclosure, has almost entirely disappeared; the central bay only remains, and this has been enclosed by mud walls and is still used as a mosque. Of the rest, all, except a few solitary blocks, has disappeared, leaving some beautifully carved *mihrābs*, or prayer niches, in the back wall, which are partly buried in accumulated debris. (Plate XLI.)

The Hindus claim the place as a Hindu building which had been appropriated by the Muḥammadans, but this is not quite correct. The building, as it now stands, is purely Muḥammadan, but, as already mentioned, it has in great part been built, as all the earlier mosques were, of pilfered material. Judging by the few columns that now remain, the whole of the pillars of the mosque were probably taken from some Hindu temple or temples; and, where the courtyard wall is broken down in places, carved temple stones and broken images may be seen built into the interior. The beautiful *mihrābs*, with their Persian inscriptions above them, are purely Musalmān work, though carried out in Hindu spirit, and, probably, by Hindu workmen. They remind one much of the designs of temple doorways. A Hindu temple possibly once existed here, and may have occupied the site on which the mosque now stands—nothing more probable—but the Hindus have now not the shadow of a claim to the place.

One of the inscriptions tells us that "The building of this Jāmi' Masjid was finished during the reign of the Defender of Islām and 'Breaker of Idols,' Jahāngir Bādshāhi G͟hāzi. May God perpetuate his kingdom! Dated the fifth month [or fifth of the month] of Zūl-Hijjah, in the fifth year of his accession" (A.D. 1610). The reference here to Jahāngir, as the breaker of idols, would seem to imply that Hindu shrines had been raided and dismantled to provide material in this case.

## MINOR MISCELLANEOUS REMAINS IN KHĀNDESH.

At Pimpalgāon Budruk, ten miles south-east of Pāchora, is the temple of Hari-Hareśvara, standing at the junction of the Bāvulā and Dabbā streams about a mile south of the village. It faces west. Though originally an old temple it has been almost entirely rebuilt with brick rubble and plaster masonry, and is now of no account architecturally. The modern finials, which are stuck upon many of these temples, are remarkable for their ugliness and inappropriateness.

Kurhād Khurd, seven miles from Māiji railway station. There is here a small old ruined temple, but it is of no particular interest. The shrine walls and part of the west walls remain. In the shrine is a *liṅga*, which, since the temple faces north, points its *śālunkā* toward the doorway.

Lohāra, fourteen miles east by north from Pāchora. The ruins of an old temple, with very plainly moulded walls, on the Sonāī stream about a mile south of the village, called Tapeśvara.

Shendurni, sixteen miles east of Pāchora, has a small ruined temple of Viśveśvara or Viśdevali. It has had an inscription covering about three feet by two feet of the outer wall on the south side, but it is too much defaced to make anything out of it. Over the shrine door is an image of Gaṇapati. Numbers of little slender pillars are inserted between the larger ones for support.

Gārkhed, eleven miles south of Bhusāval, possesses the ruins of what has once been a very fine temple of the best class. Portions, only, of the plinth and walls of the back of the shrine now remain, shewing the mouldings of the basement and a portion of the richly sculptured wall above it. For the rest. the addition of mud walls has preserved the place as the habitation of the god.

Lāling, six miles south of Dhulia. To the south of the village, by the roadside, is a small old temple, which consists of a shrine and antechamber only, the rest having been destroyed. The roof has been closed in with plaster masonry. The walls, which are for the most part original, are much weather-worn and do not appear to have been of first class workmanship.

# TEMPLES IN THE NĀSIK DISTRICT.

## SINNAR.

SINNAR, twenty miles south of Nāsik, is an ancient town, and has been mentioned in old records under the names Sindīnagara, Seuṇapura and Sindīnera. In A.D. 1025 the *Mahāsāmanta* Bhillama III of the Yādava family was ruling his hereditary province of Seuṇadesa, at his capital of Sindīnagara, as a feudatory of the Western Chālukya king Jayasiṁha II. Later, according to the *Vratakhaṇḍa* and the Bassein grant of A.D. 1069, it is recorded that Seuṇachandra I founded the town of Seuṇapura. It would appear that his son Dhadiyappa was born in the town of Sindīnera. This is about all that we know of it. According to tradition Sinnar was founded by a Gavali (Yādava) chief Rāv Shinguni about seven hundred years ago. His son Rāv Govinda is supposed to have built the great temple of Gondeśvara, or Govindeśvara, at a cost of two *lakhs* of rupees. It is possible it may be named after Govindarāja, one of the Yādava Princes, who ruled about the beginning of the 12th century. (Plates XLII—LII and LV.)

This great temple of Gondeśvara, outside the town of Sinnar on the north-east, is the largest and most complete of its class in the Dakhan. It is a *panchāyatana* temple, that is, a group of five shrines dedicated to five deities—Śiva, Vishṇu, Gaṇapati, Sūrya and Devī, the central main temple being dedicated to the first and the four small surrounding shrines to the others. Before the main entrance stands the Nandi pavilion. The buildings stand upon a long rectangular platform, the main temple in the centre and the four smaller around it, one at each corner. The whole group has been surrounded by a wall, now mostly destroyed, with two entrance porches or gateways—one on the south and one on the east—enclosing a large and ample courtyard. The great temple faces east, and the shrine contains the usual Śaivite *liṅga*. It is built of the ordinary amygdaloidal trap rock of the locality, and this has not weathered well in respect of the smaller carvings, the softer particles having disintegrated, leaving the surfaces of the exposed portions rather honeycombed.

The plan of the main building is practically the same as that of Ambarnātha, its length, over all, being 78 feet. The exteriors are also remarkably alike, the style and general disposition of the mouldings being the same. The elephant band in the basement of the Sinnar temple is bolder and far more effective than it is at Ambarnātha, but the latter has a much greater display of images on its walls. In Gondeśvara the porches are deeper and have had dwarf side walls, inside, which form benches; these did not exist in the other.

Of figure sculpture upon the temple there is very little, and what there is is chiefly confined to small images in little panels around the porches. These consist of representations of scenes from the *Rāmāyaṇa*, female dancing figures, and others of the different manifestations of the various gods and goddesses. The few images that occur upon the main walls are very poorly carved and savour much of later work than that of Ambarnātha. Little pilasters and lozenge-shaped flowers occupy, for the most part, the niches usually reserved for images. The principal images upon the temple are those upon the outside of the shrine walls. These are, above the gargoyle on the north side, and under the large niche, a four-handed *devī* or goddess, and, on the south side of the shrine, Brahmī with three faces and a goose below her. The corresponding image on the west or back of the temple has been removed. Upon each face of the temple, above these, is a deep canopied niche in which were placed the more important of the images, but they are now empty. Each has Gaja-Lakshmī above its cornice. On either side of the mass of masonry standing out before the base of the *śikhara*, that is, between the latter and the pyramidal roof of the hall, are two niches one above the other. In those on the north side of the temple are Śiva above, and what looks like Bhairava below. While the lower niche on the south side is empty, the upper one contains Śiva dancing the *tāṇḍava*. Attached to the pillars of the porches were ornamental bracket figures of females, but of these, of which there were four in each porch, two remain in the east or main porch—one very much damaged—and three in the north porch. The pilasters also had bracket figures, but they were of lions or griffins, and, of these, three remain out of six. On the whole, the images are very poorly carved and shew to very great disadvantage beside those on the small temple of Aeśvara to the north-west of the town. The ornamental gargoyle, through which the waste water from the shrine passes out, upon the north side of the temple, is, though mutilated, a particularly fine piece of work. It is in the shape of the conventional *makara* so frequently introduced into temple decoration.

The east or main porch is much damaged. The forward beam is cracked, and the immense mass of masonry above, which would otherwise collapse, is propped up by a slender square column of stone. The upper part of the parapet wall on the north side has disappeared and the forward steps and flanking masonry have been entirely renewed. The side walls of the north porch have gone, but portions of the forward steps and their flanking walls remain. The forward beam in this porch is also cracked and is propped up by the insertion of a pillar. The door lintel, too, is cracked, and is supported by two pillars, one of which, a carved pillar from elsewhere, has a curious and uncommon arrangement of foliage around its shafts, which looks like work of several centuries earlier. The flanking walls on the east side, and most of the steps of the south porch, have gone. Here, again, the forward beam has cracked and has been supported by stone props.

The ceilings of the porches are very neat, being formed of rings of cusped ornaments, with a small central pendant, which have fallen. On the face of the octagonal band, under the lowest circular moulding, are little figures, representing various scenes, such as the churning of the ocean by the gods and demons and processions. On the dedicatory blocks of all the doorways is Gaṇeśa. *Kīrti-mukha* masks and florid arabesque fill up the corners of the ceilings.

The interior of the temple is of the usual style. Four central pillars support the central dome of the ceiling, and upon them and the walls rests the whole weight of the hall roof. These four pillars, which are 9 feet 6 inches in height, are very elaborately carved, the general plan, all the way up, being square with recessed corners. The shaft, base and capital are divided up by horizontal mouldings. Among the images on the lower parts are dancers, male and female, amongst which are seen Bhairava and other deities. Higher up on the columns is a band, on the four sides of which are small groups of figures, among them being two very indecent representations. The pillar, at the north-west corner of the square, differs slightly in two of the bands about the middle of the shaft, but this is due to a flaw in the stone which necessitated their being drawn in to form a kind of neck to the pillar at that point. The pilasters are much plainer in design, all the elaborate work of the interior being concentrated upon the four pillars. These are of a very different style to those at Ambarnātha and Balsāne; they are far less graceful in outline, and the distribution of the various bands and panels of sculpture is not carried out with the same taste and eye to the general balance of parts. The spreading towards the base in the earlier pillars gives a better feeling of strength and stability. There seems to be a want of a definite plan about the sub-divisions of these columns.

The great central dome of the ceiling, which rises to a height of nearly 20 feet, is precisely like that of the porches and the antechamber—neat and chaste but not elaborate. Being so high above the beams compared with its span, and, having a deep projecting cornice round the inside of the beams, verp little light gets into the dome, which is, therefore, very dark and gloomy. The side ceilings rise in four tiers of concave cusped mouldings from the side walls to the central square.

In the walls of the hall, on either side of the entrance to the antechamber, are large framed niches for images, but these are absent. There are also larger ones in the side walls of the antechamber itself, one in each side. The beam across the entrance to the antechamber is cracked and is supported by a stone prop. The shrine doorway is of the same pattern as the outer or main doorway, being rather more elaborate than that of temple No. I at Balsāne, and a great deal more so than that of the Jaina temple at Añjaneri. Save for the clumsy threshold stone, which seems to have been an after insertion, the Balsāne doorway is a stronger and more chaste design than the Sinnar one. In this, the pilasters, on either side, which support the cornice, are less prominently marked, and are more or less lost in the group of mouldings which surrounds it. The *kīrtimukha* face, which is, as a rule, found upon the threshold, does not occur here. The interior of the shrine is plain, the floor being on the same level as the hall floor; and in the middle of it is a large *liṅga*. The present Nandi, in the Nandi pavilion, appears to be a comparatively new one; another one about the same size, with the headless fragments of two others, lie below on the pavement.

It is difficult now to say, with absolute certainty, to what deities the four surrounding shrines were dedicated, but, judging from the sculptures which remain upon them, the nort-west one was assigned to Pārvatī, the south-west to Gaṇapati, the north-east to Sūrya, and the south-east to Vishṇu. Among the smaller images, around the Nandi pavilion, are two of the *avatāras* of Vishṇu, namely, Varāha and Narasiṁha.

The *śikhara* has lost its own finial and has been capped with an incongruous Muhammadan dome in brick and mortar, which is to be removed. The small shrines have also lost the whole or part of their finials. hat the original was like may be seen, to some extent, in the photographs of the temples at Jhodgā and Ratanvādi. The masonry of the roof of the hall, shown in black in the section, is built hollow, and the main tower is also hollow above the shrine ceiling.

The temple of Āeśvara, upon the north-west of the town, just above the rivulet, is in the Chālukyan style and, so, does not belong to the class of work usually found in the Dakhan. It is the most northerly Chālukyan structure that has been found. Nothing is known of its origin, and even tradition gives us no clue to the reason for it being found so far north of its natural habitat.

Fig. 9—The temple of Āeśvara, looking towards the shrine.

It has the appearance of a temple of the best period of Chālukyan work, that is, about the eleventh century, and is possibly older than that of Gondēśvara. There are some details it seems to have borrowed from the northern style, such as, for instance, the *kichaka* bracket above the capital of the pillars—the little squat figure in the act of supporting the beam. This is not found in Chālukyan work. [1]

The temple, as it stands, consists of a shrine, with nearly the whole of its tower missing, and two groups of four pillars standing out in front of the shrine, which formed part of a long hall, or two halls, one in advance of the other. These retain their beams above them. There were enclosing walls around these, which is shewn by parts of their foundations which still remain (Plate LV). There was also a raised platform around the shrine as the indented outline for the elephant moulding of its foundation shows. There would appear to have been images in the recesses between the pilasters all around the shrine walls, but they have been removed. The group of pillars, nearest the shrine, are octagonal in plan with recessed corners, but of the outer group of four, the inner two are six-sided in plan, and the outer pair are square. There are three very ornamental niches in the base of the shrine, one on each side.

Among the images still remaining on the outside of the temple, which are all small, is a *devī* (Pārvatī ?) seated upon a tiger or a lion with curly mane up above the cornice on the south face. Little corner lion-brackets occupy the tops of the wall pilasters while, between them, in the running band, are small figures of sorts, some of which are very indecent. Around the lower part of the wing walls, a portion of which remains on the north side, there have been some very fine carved groups, some of which have been carried away and have been built into the wall of a little shrine on the bank of the stream near by. A fragment of one of these groups still exists in the north wing wall, west face, with two on the north face representing incidents from the *Rāmāyaṇa*, the other being a group of three standing figures in an attitude of adoration.

A most superb piece of carving overarches the entrance to the antechamber. Forming a semicircular arch are three bands, the centre one of little dancing dwarfs. These rise from the jaws of two *makaras*, one on either side, with the most wonderful tails of flowing arabesque, which turn up over their backs and forward on to the arched bands. The central semicircular panel, under the arch, is occupied by a representation of Śiva dancing the *tāṇḍava*. A musician on his left keeps time on his drum, and Pārvatī sits on his right amazed at his performance. Three wedge-shaped slots in the stone, under this sculpture, show that another slab had been slipped on below which probably was a sculptured band containing Śiva's *gaṇa*.

The ceiling of the antechamber is flat, and is divided by deep cross bars into nine sunk squares, in each of which was a group of figures, but the central one has been destroyed. The remaining represent the *ashṭadikpālas* or the regents of the eight points of the compass. This is a very favourite ceiling in Chālukyan

[1] Compare the walls and pillars with those in the temple of Malikārjuna at Kuruvaṭṭi, and with some of the pillars in Nannesvara at Lakkundi. *The Chālukyan Architecture of the Kanarese Districts*, plates LXXIII and CVIII.

temples and has been fully described in a previous volume.[1] The sculptor has, however, made a blunder in putting Agni, on his ram, in the north compartment which should have contained Kuvera, on his horse. Kuvera is probably in the wrong place in the south-east corner where Agni ought to be, but this sculpture is damaged beyond all recognition. The regents should be as follows :—

| | |
|---|---|
| N. Kuvera on the horse. | S. Yama on the male buffalo. |
| N-E. Iśa on the bull. | S-W. Nirṛiti on a man. |
| E. Indra on the elephant. | W. Varuṇa on a *makara*. |
| S-E. Agni on the ram. | N-W. Vāyu on the deer. |

Above the shrine doorway, which is fairly well decorated, is a line of figures representing the *saptamātṛis* or the "Seven Mothers," another sculpture peculiar to Chālukyan temples, since the members of the Chālukya family were under the special guardianship of these divine mothers. There are, however, eleven figures in the row. On the left side is Śiva with a standing attendant, and on the right, Gaṇapati and Śiva as Bhairava. On the dedicatory block we find the Chālukyan Gaja-Lakshmī instead of Gaṇapati who is the favourite presiding deity among the Dekhan temples. Occupying the middle of the band of mouldings, immediately above this, is Vishṇu upon Śesha. On the lower inner face of the south antechamber pilaster is Brahmā, Vishṇu occupying the north one. On the outer pilasters are *dvārapālas* or door-keepers. The larger female figures on the pillars have been well carved, and exhibit exceptional elegance of pose. Among the smaller figures are some of the *avatāras* of Vishṇu. The interior of the shrine is perfectly plain, and a *liṅga* now occupies the centre of the floor.

In addition to the temples just described, there are two other old ones in the village of no particular interest, save that one has four doors to its shrine. It has the usual *maṇḍapa* or hall before it, into which one door enters, but the doors in the other three walls of the shrine lead out into the open. The shrine walls are complete with all their mouldings on the outside shewing that there was no other enclosing wall beyond it, and, therefore no *pradakshina* to which the doors could have led. There may have been porches before each of these. Above the door leading into the hall is Gaṇapati, but above the others there are no images. The *liṅga* now occupies the shrine.

Out in the fields, about a mile east of the town, is a small "Hemāḍpanti" shrine which is partly in ruins.

Just outside the east gate, by a well, were two Jaina images, each of them being a colossal figure of a female seated on a tiger. These were half buried in the earth.

## JHODGA.

Jhodgā is about seventy-five miles to the north-east of Nāsik on the borders of Khāndesh. At the foot of a small hill, to the west of the town, is a well-finished old temple of Mahādeva, which looks exceedingly well as it stands out in the open, without any surroundings, upon its high basement. It consists of a central hall with its porch and three shrines, the main *śikhara* being all but complete. The whole is richly wrought and decorated. The

[1] *The Chālukyan Architecture of the Kanarese Districts.*

main shrine, hall and porch are of original construction, but the two side shrines are of later and inferior workmanship, and no attempt has been made on these to preserve the lines of mouldings which run round the older work. It is possible the side shrines were not in the original plan, but had been added in the place of porches. This alteration made the interior very dark, and so four irregular rectangular openings were made in the side walls to let in a little light. These appear to have been made by knocking out the most convenient blocks of stone from the walling. The temple faces the west, and Gaṇapati presides above the shrine doorway. (Plates LIII—LVI.)

The style of tower, and the mouldings of the outer walls, closely resemble those of Gondeśvara at Sinnar, and the more complete top with the little finials in the wall ornament, enable us to reconstruct the top of the *śikhara* at Sinnar. The *kīrtimukha* faces at the top of the tower are replaced by human faces in later temples. The face of the projection on the front of the tower is carved into an elaborate arrangement of *kīrtimukhas* and arched scrolls of arabesque. In a panel, in the centre, is a six-handed seated image. The lower hands rest in the lap, but the upper hands and the head have been destroyed. Below this is a row of niches, in the centre one of which, judging from the general outline of the fractured surface, was Śiva, probably dancing the *tāṇḍava*. On his left are the remains of a standing figure, with one of its left hands across its chest as if holding a flute to its mouth, as Kṛishṇa is usually represented, while below is a small kneeling figure—perhaps, Garuḍa—with head and shoulders destroyed. On the right of Śiva was a figure which has disappeared all but one foot, but the goose, below, shows that it was Brahmā. Thus we have the traid of gods who are flanked, on either side, by a female *chauri* bearer. Beneath this line of figures, in the centre, is a small rectangular opening into the hollow of the *śikhara*, which does not appear ever to have been used as a shrine; it has no dedicatory image over it, nor has it any door-frame.

A curious thing about this temple is that it has no framed doorway to the hall, the entrance being the whole width between the pilasters in front.

The temple is decorated with a greater number of images than that of Gondeśvara at Sinnar, and these are chiefly confined to the walls of the shrine. On the east, or back of the shrine, the principal niche is empty. Above, on the base of the *śikhara*, is Indra seated with his elephant beneath him. On the north side, the principal niche contains the *tāṇḍava*, but the legs and arms are broken off; the image on the base of the *śikhara*, above, is gone. On the south side, the principal niche contains Bhairava, while, above him on the *śikhara*, is Yama on his buffalo. These upper niches, therefore, contained the regents of the points of the compass which they face. In addition to these, other panels and corners of the walls are filled with images, singly or in pairs, such as musicians, female dancers, the *dikpālas*, Mahiśāsura-mardanī, several times repeated, Mahākālī, and warriors with round and rectangular shields.

The interior of the temple is comparatively simple and plain. One large domical ceiling covers in the *maṇḍapa* which is unsupported by any intermediate pillars. The dome rises in a series of thirteen concentric circles of mouldings, in the usual manner, to the apex, from which a pendant hung at one time. About half way up, is a ring of eight bracket figures, which are now much damaged. The eight pillars at the main entrance and the entrances to the antechambers, are very clumsy and do not match the pilasters: they appear to be an addition made subsequently to the building of the temple. The beam above the entrance to the principal antechamber is cracked, and the failure of this was probably the reason for introducing them throughout. As the columns now leave very little unsupported space beneath the beams, the cracked one could hardly have given way after their insertion.

The ceiling of the antechamber is rectangular, and rises in diminishing rectangles, the mouldings being somewhat similar to those of the hall ceiling. The shrine doorway is fairly well decorated, but the work is a trifle coarse, in fact the work on the whole temple is not of the first class.

The only original free-standing pillars in the temple are the two in the entrance porch.

In the side shrines low altars have been placed, upon which were set up small *piṇḍis*. Out in front of the porch, upon a roughly raised platform, which may be all that is left of a pavilion, is a large mutilated Nandi, looking towards the shrine.

About a hundred yards to the west, or front, of this temple is the shrine and antechamber of a smaller one, of plainer design. There is nothing of interest about it except a curious little panel sculpture on the back representing a two-leaved door surmounted by the *chaitya*-window ornament.

## ANJANERĪ.

The village of Añjanerī is picturesquely situated on the eastern slope of the northern spur of Añjanerī or Añjanī Hill, about fourteen miles west of Nāsik. Just below the village, in the plain, scattered over an area of about half a square mile, there have been innumerable small shrines, of which sixteen now stand in whole or in part, while the rest are represented by mounds upon which lie heaps of their material—columns, images, beams and other carved stones. The most striking feature about these remains is that they all appear to have been built upon a small scale, and they are independent temples and not satelites to a larger one. They all seem to rest upon brick foundations, and have been dedicated to various deities, the more important being Jaina, two Vaishnava, and the rest Śaiva. They face all four points of the compass. They are not now used, nor do they appear to have been much used at any time; and the shattered condition they are now in points rather to wanton destruction at the hands of man than the ravages of time; trees, cactus bushes, and other plants still grow luxuriantly upon them. In addition to the temples there have been extensive masonry tanks, little of which, except their pits and a few bits of stonework, remains. (Plates LVII—LXI.)

There is one group of shrines which, on account of their better preservation than the rest, and that in one of them is a finely engraved and important inscription, might be considered the principal group. This cluster contains six distinct buildings, which, at some time subsequent to the erection of the last, have been surrounded by a wall with an entrance gateway on the south. The largest, which we may call No. 1, faces the east and, like No. 5 at Balsāne, has an open front and verandah; in fact, they all have this open verandah in place of a porch. It consists of the shrine, with a pillared hall before it, and a deep pillared verandah before this again. The exterior of the temple is remarkably plain, the only decoration being a series of simple mouldings with a few fretwork bands running round it. This peculiar style of surface ornament, which takes the place of the panels and figure bands in the earlier examples, is seen more developed in the temples at Ratanvādi and Sangameśvara, and, combined with figures, in Chāngdeva and Tahākāri. The *śikhara* is in the northern style, but is plain, the main features being only blocked out.

Within the shrine was an altar or seat, against the back wall, upon which, no doubt, an image of a Jina was placed. Only the lower part of this now remains, the rest of it lies about the shrine and hall, it having been wantonly destroyed. Upon the dedicatory blocks of both the shrine and hall doorways is a seated Jina, that on the outer one being flanked by images of Parśvanātha, while that on the shrine doorway is flanked by *devīs*. The central bay of the verandah ceiling is domical and has a neat eight-pointed rosette pendent from the centre. The side ceilings are oblong, and are just sections of the side ceilings in the hall. The central bay of the hall ceiling is similar to that of the verandah, but more lofty. The antechamber has a plain oval, rising in two tiers, the oval being rather flat. It is like those in the temples at Sangameśvara and Chāngdeva, and is very unusual. Being rather dumpy in outline it is not a success.

On either side of the doorway, in the verandah, is a niche for an image, but they are now empty. The floors of most of these temples have been upturned, probably by the Muḥammadans in search of treasure.

The pillars are after the style of those at Pāṭna, the *kīrtimukha* mask forming a conspicuous detail in their decoration, and they have no images upon them. Notwithstanding that this is a Jaina temple, the doorway has the *kīrtimukha* upon its threshold, one on either side of the centre projection. The female images at the foot of the jambs, holding waterpots, are probably intended for the river goddesses Gangā and Yamunā who occupy this position in the very early temples. The two large images of Parśvanātha, above the door, indicate, no doubt, that the temple was dedicated to that *tīrthankara*.

Temple No. 2, which stands at right angles to the last and close to it, was perhaps, the most important in the group, since it contains a slab bearing an interesting inscription. It is smaller than No. 1, but in other respects it is very similar to it. It has no pillars in the hall, the small size of the building not making them necessary. The two pillars in the porch, or verandah, are rather more ornate than those in temple No. 1, and approach more nearly to those of temple No. 2 at Balsāne, being almost counterparts of them.

Before the hall doorway is a very prettily designed low step or *ardhachandra*. The altar and the flooring of the shrine have been destroyed; the doorway is like the outer one in the last temple, having two standing Parśvanātha images above it. Two large mutilated Jinas are lying in the hall—one a seated image with the top of the head knocked off, and the other a nude image of Parśvanātha. It was thus a Digambara shrine. It faces the south.

The inscribed slab is set up on the side wall of the hall, above a niche. It is not built into the wall, but rather against it, being gripped and held in position between the beam above and the top of the cornice of the niche; and since the top of this niche is five inches lower than that of the niche on the other side, in order to allow of the insertion of the slab; it is likely the slab was put up when the temple was built. It records the gift of three shops in the city (probably Añjanerī) for the upkeep of the temple of Chandraprabha by the king Seuṇachandra III in *Śaka* 1063 (A. D. 1142). It further records that a rich merchant, named Vatsarāja, with two others, gave a shop and a house for the same purpose.

There can be little doubt but that this temple was built before No. 1 for one would hardly expect to find a king settling gifts upon the lesser of two temples standing side by side.

Of temple No. 3 only the verandah and part of the west wall of the hall remain, the rest being completely wrecked. The pillars and walls are very plain and the doorway even more so. On the block, above the latter, is a seated Jina. It faces north.

Buildings No. 4, 5 and 6 in this group were, perhaps, rather *mathas* or rest houses than temples. They have no shrines, and the halls of Nos. 4 and 6 are oblong. Four pillars support the hall ceilings in each case, and each has a verandah in front. The central ceiling of No. 4 is flat, and is decorated with three circular rosettes. Thin slender pillars were inserted between the forward and back pairs of the pillars of the hall, to assist in supporting the extra long beams above, but only one of these still stands; part of another lies on the floor. Only one pillar of the verandah stands; the rest, with the whole of the roof, has fallen. The building faces the south. Nos. 5 and 6, which face the east, are in ruins.

About fifty yards south of the last group is another small Jaina temple No. 7, which is very plainly built. The shrine doorway, which is very simple in design, has a Jina upon the block but no work above the cornice. The pillars have plain square shafts with simply moulded bases and caps, and a few only remain. Beside this one, on the north, has been another Jaina shrine or *matha*, like Nos. 5 and 6, but nothing now stands except the doorway and a part of the adjacent wall. The whole appears to have had an enclosing wall of some extent around it.

No. 8, which is a small Vaishṇava shrine, built and sculptured in the same style as that of Gondeśvara at Sinnar, is about a hundred yards to the west of the last temple and nearer the village. Only the shrine of the temple is now standing. The three principal images on the outside of the shrine are—on the east, Varāha, on the south Narasiṁha, and on the west the Vāmana *avatāra*. In the shrine, against the back wall, is a low altar, on the front of which is Garuḍa, and over the shrine door are Śiva, Vishṇu and Brahmā, Vishṇu being in the middle. The image upon the dedicatory block above the shrine doorway has been much mutilated, but it was probably Garuḍa. The antechamber ceiling is, in plan, lentoid or a pointed oval which is a very unusual shape. The temple faces north.

Twenty to thirty yards to the west of the last is No. 9, a small plainly built temple, of which the shrine and *śikhara* remain, all except the *kalaśa* or finial, the hall being completely ruined. Above the shrine door is Gaṇapati. There are the remains of what seems to have been an altar, with a weather-worn image carelessly placed upon it. The temple faces east.

No. 10 is about twenty to thirty yards to the north of the last, under a large banyan tree. It is the wreck of a small Jaina temple. Over the shrine doorway is a Jina, while sitting in the midst of this desolation, presiding over the ruins, is a much weatherworn life-sized Jina, sitting now in the open air, the shrine walls having fallen. The temple faces the east. Behind this shrine is a high rocky mound, having upon it some small memorial stones, set up in a line facing west, and daubed with red paint.

About four hundred yards due north of the first group of temples (Nos. 1 to 6) is a little shrine, No. 11, with its *śikhara* and antechamber, but without its hall, which has been ruined. It is plainly built, but has a good sculptured doorway to the shrine, with Gaṇapati on the dedicatory block. The shrine is empty. The temple faces east, and has an inscription of one line upon a pilaster.

A hundred and fifty yards east-north-east of the last are two small shrines (No. 12), the northern one of which is much shattered. The principal images upon its walls are the *tāṇḍava* (?), Gaṇapati, and Mahākālī, and Gaṇapati figures, again, above the shrine door. In the shrine, against the back wall, is an altar with Garuḍa on the front, which has probably been brought from some other temple. Loosely placed upon it are images of Śiva-Pārvatī, Narasiṁha and Vishṇu (?). The temple faces east. About ten yards to the south of the last is No. 13, a plain, square little shrine, with a pyramidal roof, facing west.

These last two shrines appear to have stood upon the edge of a large masonry tank, and, at a distance of seventy to eighty yards to the north-west of them, is a length of about ten yards of old masonry steps of the tank still remaining. Down below these temples, in what was the bed of the tank, was a mutilated boar similar to that at Balsāne, but it has only four small figures upon it—two forward and two aft. A large figure, however, stands beside the left shoulder of the boar with the right arm turned upward toward its snout which has been mutilated. This is, of course, a representation of the boar *avatāra* of Vishṇu, which, on a colossal scale, is seen at Erān in the Central Provinces.

About three hundred yards east of the last, on the south-west corner of what was once a tank, but now a rice field, are the ruins of another small shrine (No. 14) which faces east. A *liṅga* lies half buried in the shrine. In front of it, on the south side of the tank, are the sites of two other small shrines.

Nos. 15 and 16 are about half a mile east of the village, at the foot of some low hills. They are the ruins of two small buildings, one being a temple and the other probably a *maṭha*. In addition to the above, there are the sites of many more buildings, which are now represented by mounds scattered about the fields, upon which still lie, in many cases, sculptured stones, columns and images.

Beside the temples in the plain, there are sundry remains upon Añjanerī hill. Upon the very highest plateau, 4,300 feet above sea level, and some 2,000 feet above the temples just described, is a small roughly-built temple dedicated to the goddess Añjinī, who is here represented by the usual red-bedaubed rough stone image. The material of which this shrine has been built belonged to a previous temple of a more pretentious design. In the upper cliff to the north-east, just above the pond and bungalows, is a small roughly-hewn Jaina cave. A small doorway, with coarse figures on either side, gives access to a long verandah room, off the back of which is the shrine with a roughly-cut Jina seated within. In the lower cliff, in the side of the gorge through which the rough ascent passes, is another small Jaina cave with its sculpture better finished than in the one above. Parśvanātha flanks the doorways. Like the temples below, these caves belong to the Digambara Jains. Attached to the cave is a water cistern.

## DEVALĀNĀ.

The village of Devalānā is fifty-six miles north-east of Nāsik. There is here an old three-shrined temple dedicated to Jāgeśvara; but the three shrines, like the side ones at Jhodgā, have been rebuilt in a very plain manner. A few courses of the basement of the old building remain below the later work, which show that, like the porch, it was elaborately decorated. As will be seen from the plan, the front of the hall is open, its eaves and corners being supported upon dwarf pillars which stand upon the low parapet wall, An image of Śiva is placed in a niche on either side of the entrance, and, among the smaller ones round the parapet wall, are some very indecent pairs. The hall has a central circular panel of sculpture portraying Kṛishṇa and the *gopīs*, like the one in the Mānbhāvā temple at Vāghlī. There is also a panel of three medallions, the centre one of which is worked into a design of *Nāgas* whose rope-like tails are intertwined and knotted in a most complicated manner. The pillars are somewhat like those at Añjanerī. (Plates LXII and LXIII.)

## TRINGALVADI.

Though not a built structure, the interesting rock-cut Jaina temple near the village of Tringalvādi, is included in our account of the Dakhan shrines since it has not been noticed in our previous volumes on the cave-temples, not having then been examined. Tringalvādi is six miles north-west of Igatpurī, the railway station at the top of the Thal Ghāt, the cave being cut in the foot of the hillside, about a mile west of the village. Though now much the worse for centuries of weathering, it was once a very ornate cave-temple. (Plate LXIV.)

FIG. 10.—Pillar in the hall of Tringalvādi cave.

It consists of a large hall, 35 feet square, off the back of which are an antechamber and a shrine, and before it is a long verandah the full length of the width of the hall. Along the front of this verandah is a low parapet wall from which rise two pillars, one on either side of the entrance, supporting the outer eave of the verandah. Opposite these pillars are pilasters, and, between the latter, is the main doorway into the hall. Beyond these pilasters, and between them and each end of the verandah, is a grille window—two square bars each way dividing it into nine lights. The front of these bars is prettily chased with lotus rosettes at the junctions.

In the centre of the verandah ceiling, and in front of the doorway, hanging in deep relief, is a group of five figures in a circle. The middle figure appears to be assisted or carried through the air by another on either side, while two others, beneath, also help. Over the doorway, upon the dedicatory block, is a Jina.

The hall ceiling was supported upon four columns set square in the middle of the hall. The walls and ceiling are plain. Round the two sides of the south-west and north-west corners are very low continuous altars for images while round the two sides of the north-east and south-east corners are high benches which are not altars. The south-east pillar, only, remains intact (Fig. 10); the south-west one is continuous from floor to ceiling, but is much corroded about the middle. The north-west and north-east pillars have completely gone, fragments hanging from the ceiling, and their stumps on the floor, being all that is left of them.

The shrine doorway is much disintegrated, but it was not so elaborately decorated as the front door. Over it, one above the other on three bands of mouldings, are three Jinas. Within the shrine, which is quite plain, measuring 13 by 12 feet, are the remains of a Jaina image upon an altar placed against the back wall. The chest, head and umbrella have been smashed and thrown away—part of the umbrella lies outside the cave—but the legs and the cushion are left. On the middle of the cushion is the bull, showing that the image was that of a Ṛishabdeva, while on either side of it is an inscription dated Saka 1266.

There was a very fine inscription upon the wall in the north end of the cave, but only a very small fragment of it remains. The letters are small and well shaped. The inscribed surface seems to have been about four to five feet across, but it is not certain how deep. The front of the cave with the main doorway was originally painted, traces of which still remain. The partition wall, between the verandah and the hall, has been entirely built of great irregular blocks of stone well fitted together.

## CHĀNDOR.

At the town of Chāndor, some thirty-eight miles to the north-east of Nāsik, are a Jaina cave and the modern temple of Renukā Devī; and, on the hill fort of Indrāi, not far off, is a range of thirteen small rooms cut in the rock.

The temple of Renukā Devī is quite a modern building and would not be noticed here were it not for two curious wooden images found at it. There is one feature, however, connected with the temple, which may be mentioned, and that is the fine broad flight of steps leading up to it. At the foot of this is a collection of miniature flights of steps, of five steps each, carved on small square loose blocks of stone, which have been left here by pilgrims as votive offerings, but with what object it is not clear. (Plates LXIV—LXVI.)

The wooden images, bedaubed with red paint and much weatherworn, were found lying in the inner courtyard. They are worshipped by the people under the names of Kharujāli and Mahāmārī. An examination of them shows that they are Roman Catholic images, probably taken from some old ruined church in or about Sālsette. "Mahāmārī" (? Mahā-Marie) is a representation of the Annunciation, in which the Virgin Mary stands upon a crescent moon with a crown upon her head and clothed in flowing garments. Around her, forming an oval frame, is a garland of flowers. The other image is that of St. Anne, with the infant Mary upon her knee. The first was probably a panel in a church door or screen, while the second is a complete statue which may have come from a niche.

The Jaina cave, which is excavated in one of the lower cliffs of the Chāndor fort hill, just above the town to the east, is a roughly-cut small room entered by a single doorway and supported, within, by two heavy clumsily-cut square columns. Around the sides of the cave are scores of images, large and small, most of them being those of the *tīrthankaras*. On the back, or west wall, is the principal image, that of Chandrāprabha, with the crescent moon carved below him. Upon the pilaster, on either side of him, are two little groups of the twenty-four *tīrthankaras*. Beyond these are the two images so frequently met with in Jaina caves—the man on an elephant on the one side and the woman on a tiger, beneath a tree, on the other. Very fine images of these two are found in the Indrā Sabha cave at Elūra, where they are known as Indra and Indrani. They possibly represent some great local patron of the Jaina religion and his wife. Such portrait statues are common in Gujarāt temples—the statues of Vastupāla and Tejpāla, and their wives, in the famous marble temples of Dilwara at Mt. Abu for instance. At the top of the pilasters, on either side of Chandrāprabha, is a small image of Sarasvatī. Parśvanātha also figures upon the walls. Upon the south wall of the cave are images of Sarasvatī and a four-armed *Devī*. These are red-leaded and worshipped, the latter as Kālikā Mātā, dirty bits of cloth being wound about her to represent her garments. On the floor, midway between the two pillars, is a tortoise in low relief.

Near the top of the ascent to this cave, where the way leads up some rock-cut steps, are some miniatute steps cut out in the rock, similar to the little votive steps at Renukā's temple. In the rock, a little higher up the hill-side, is a water cistern.

In the top of Indrāi fort, above the upper cliffs, towards the north end and facing east, is a row of thirteen caves varying from twelve to twenty feet square. They are in a continuous row, being separated from one another by thin partition walls. Each has its doorway, two windows, and verandah, and, in front of one, the largest, about the middle of the line, are two pillars supporting the outer eave of the verandah. In the middle of each of three of the partition walls is a doorway connecting the two adjacent caves. There is nothing about these excavations to indicate for what use they were intended; the absence of images would show that they were probably not used for religious purposes. They were possibly intended to afford shelter to a garrison in ancient times.

Of the history of Chāndor we know little or nothing beyond the fact, gathered from a copper-plate grant, that the first Yādava king, Dṛiḍhaprahāra had Chandrādityapura (Chāndor) as his capital.

# TEMPLES IN THE AHMADNAGAR DISTRICT

## KOKAMTHĀN.

THE village of Kokamthān, about fifty-six miles north of Ahmadnagar, is situated upon the right bank of the Godāverī, some three miles to the south-east of Kopargāon, a station on the railway. Built upon what appears to be an artificial embankment, projecting into the stream bed upon the north-east outskirts of the village, is a very interesting old temple. It consists of the usual shrine and *maṇḍapa* with two porches, one on the west side of the hall and one on the north, directly opposite the shrine. A small additional shrine takes the place of a porch upon the east side of the *maṇḍapa*. The building has been designed upon a star-shaped plan, which, however, is rather obscured by the three heavy square buttresses around the shrine, and by the porches and the square side shrine of the hall which break the star-planned corners. It is possible that the side shrine of the hall is a later addition, the outer walls, in their treatment, being so very unlike the rest. Had this been part of the original plan, it would, like temple No. 1 at Balsāne, have been carried out in precisely the same style, the same mouldings and panelling being carried around its walls. Like the temples at Jodghā and Devalānā, this shrine has taken the place of a porch which stood opposite the one on the west of the hall. Above the doorways of the two porches, as well as above that of the main shrine, is Garuḍa; which, coupled with the fact that the temple faces the north, shows clearly that it was originally a Vaishṇava temple. But above the doorway of this small shrine is Gaṇapati, which is in favour of it being built as a Śaiva shrine, probably when the temple fell into the hands of that sect. (Plates LXVII—LXIX.)

Applied to the three sides of the shrine, outside, are three heavy buttresses, which, since they are not necessitated by any wall shrines within, must have been added in order to strengthen the walls under the great pressure of the lofty tower which rose above them. These are designed in keeping with the walls and tower of the temple itself. The mouldings are the same though on a miniature scale; and from these it can be seen what the top of the tower, which is now absent, must have been like. These are, without doubt, original work, and were provided for in the original plan. Perhaps the inferior quality of the stone used caused the builders to be doubtful of the ability of the walls to carry the weight of the superstructure.

The lower part of the building, that is, the walls between the ground line and the cornice, is built of stone, but the tower above this, and the roof of the *maṇḍapa*, are built of brick, the whole of which, both stone and brick, having been plastered. The ornament and figures, which had been first carved in stone, have been overlaid with plaster, in which their outlines and forms have been reproduced. On the brickwork the whole of the decorative detail has been formed solely in the plaster, and, in this respect, differs from the older brick temples, such as that at Śirpur in the Central Provinces, where the ornament was first executed in the brick before being overlaid. It was a common thing in the Dakhan, in temples of this age and later, to build them partly in stone and partly in brick, and the plaster upon the stonework was probably intended to bring the whole to one uniform appearance. In the photograph the one is indistinguishable from the other.

The front, or north, porch has a plain spiral ceiling similar to that in the porch in the north end of the *Jāmi' masjid* at Ahmadābād, but with less decoration.[1] It is now a good deal the worse for weathering. In the west porch is a cusped ceiling somewhat similar to those in the Jāmi' Masjid at Broach,[2] but not so elaborate as the best of those.

The principal object of worship in the shrine, at present, is the *linga;* but, behind it, resting against the wall, is a slab bearing an image of Vishṇu reclining upon Śesha, which is set up on end. The beams which stand forward from the four walls of the shrine are supported upon intervening brackets or consoles, in addition to the walls and corner pilasters. The shrine floor is on the same level as the floor of the hall. The doorway is fairly well carved, and is of the usual style, with a little florid centre piece under the cornice, as at Pedgāon. Five *devīs* occupy as many small niches in a line above the door cornice.

In the wall, on either side of the antechamber, is a niche for an image. The antechamber ceiling is domical, rising in plain concave and concentric mouldings to a central rosette, which falls again as a pendant in two tiers of cusped mouldings.

The side shrine, off the hall, which is smaller than the principal one, has a low altar at the back, upon which there is now a rather shapeless stone which may have been the slab which once bore an image. It is daubed with red paint and is called by the villagers Jagadambā Devī.

The central hall has no free-standing pillars, the ceiling being worked up from the pilasters, which are generally square in plan. Heavy architraves form an octagon of unequal sides, from which the domical ceiling rises in rings of concave mouldings to a central pendent rosette, which again falls as a finial. Each group of cup-shaped cusped mouldings, in the three tiers of the pendant has a separate drop or finial of its own. These drops, with the central one, were fitted in as separate stones, some of which are missing. There are eight figure brackets around the inside of the dome, six of which hold dancing figures, the little squat figures below being musicians.

---

[1] *Ahmadābād Architecture*, by Dr. Jas. Burgess, Part I, plate XXXVII.

[2] *Gujarāt Architecture*, by Dr. Jas. Burgess, plates X—XVI.

## AKOLA.

The sleepy little town of Akolā, with its steep narrow streets paved with cobbles, and old *vādās* or mansions now falling into decay, is built upon the bank of the Pravarā river some sixty miles to the north-west of Aḥmadnagar. To the east of the town, a little distance above the bank of the river, is the old temple of Siddheśvara. It is said that the temple was buried in the silt of the river, until about 1780, when a *kunbi's* plough struck against the *kalaśa* of the spire. If it had been buried, it must have been under the gradual accumulation of earth washed down by the rains from the hillocks that overtop it on the south. Its basement is at present buried to a depth of about four feet on the side of the hillocks and some two feet on the opposite.

FIG. 11.—Pillar in the temple of Siddhesvara.

The style of the temple is that of the temple of Baleśvara at Pedgaon, the walls being comparatively plain when compared with the more highly sculptured shrine. But the most interesting feature of this temple are the two doorways to the sanctum—the usual one leading from the hall, and a second opposite to it in the back wall, leading out into the open. This is peculiar and very unusual.[1] It is a Śaiva temple dedicated to the worship of the *liṅga*, and appears always to have been so. It faces the west. (Plates LXX—LXXIII.)

The general plan consists of the *maṇḍapa* or hall, entered through a porch on the west, with an antechamber and shrine on the east of it, and a porch, again, before the eastern, or back door, of the shrine. On the north and south sides of the hall, forming wings to it, are porch-like extensions, but having no exit. They are walled in all around with a low dwarf wall, from which rise dwarf pillars supporting the overhanging cornice above, and leaving the space between the wall and the cornice open.

[1] Further up this valley, at the village of Ratanvādi, is an old temple which, like this, has an extra door to the shrine through the back wall. At Sinnar, in the village, is another old temple with four doors to the shrine, which has already been noticed. The old temple of Siddhanātha at Mandhātā, in the Narmadā, has a shrine with four doors, but, in this case, the shrine is the central feature of the general plan, which is that of a Greek cross, the arms being the porches in front of the doors. One other shrine, with four doors, is that in the village of Unkal, in the Dhārwār District, described in my volume on Chālukyan architecture. This last is of the same plan as that at Sinnar.

The whole of the roofing of the temple, excepting the ceiling of the eastern porch, is of late work from the beams upwards. When these repairs were carried out the walls were "pointed" with mortar where no mortar existed before; and these raw white lines do not improve the appearance of the building. Five roughly-shaped columns, shewn in the plan in hatched lines, have been inserted to support cracked beams. The small pillars, placed between the four large ones, and in the middle of the sides of the north and south extensions, are seemingly original and in their original positions. The inner faces of the beams, in the central bay of the hall ceiling, are sculptured with bands of figures in relief. Upon the east beam the churning of the ocean is portrayed. Holding on to the tail of the serpent are twelve male figures, while but one male figure holds the head, beyond which are three female figures seated, and a horse and an elephant, the products of the churning. Between the three female figures and the man who holds the elephant, is an unoccupied stool towards which the female figures turn in an attitude of supplication. Over the west beam is Vishṇu on Śesha, with four Nāga figures on one side and five on the other, while, beyond them, stand men in rows holding garlands. On the south beam is a battle scene with horses and elephants and camels.[1] Upon the north beam is a procession, in which the principal figure is carried in a *pālki*, with horsemen and elephant before, and a file of men with swords and shields behind. On either side of the antechamber is a deep framed niche, now empty. Except for these the walls of the temple inside are quite plain.

The shrine doorways are fairly well decorated, both being alike; upon the block above the doorways is Gaṇapati. The entrance doorway to the hall on the west, together with its porch, have been entirely rebuilt, the side jambs and threshold, only, of the original being included in the new work. The shrine floor is lower than the rest, and a step from the doorway leads down to it, where, in the centre, and sunk within it, is the *liṅga*. The Nandi, instead of being in front of the temple on the west, is placed in front of the back, or east doorway, of the shrine.

Upon the outside of the shrine walls, on the north and the south, is a niche. In the south one is a representation of the *tanḍava* of Śiva, while in the north one is Kālikā-Mātā, or Mahākālī, as a skeleton dancing upon a prostrate figure, but both are much mutilated. Round the outside of the low walls of the porches are little figures in recesses between miniature pilasters. These are not well carved, having large heads and goggle eyes. Two of these, on the east side of the north porch, have been enclosed in a little arched masonry recess, and have been well smeared with red paint. They are Gaṇeśa and Mahākālī.

There are four much worn *viragals*, or hero stones, on the south, and one on the north side of the temple, and not far from it.

---

[1] The camel is very rarely seen represented upon early Hindu temples. It occurs upon the temple at the Hirā gateway at Dabhoi, and on two of the later temples at Chitorgarh.

The portion of a pillar bearing an inscription, mentioned in the *Indian Antiquary*,[1] is in the old *kacheri* enclosure before the Subordinate Judge's court. The letters are almost entirely obliterated. Above the writing are represented the sun and the moon. The stone, which is a pilaster, does not appear to have belonged to this temple. Mr. Sinclair, writing of this temple, said, "unfortunately the front porch has been restored, by some pious blockhead in the Saracenic style of a handsome modern temple in the village, so that it is not available for purposes of comparison. More than that the Vandal threw away the ruins of the old porch, on one of which was a long Sanskrit inscription observed, but not copied, by Dr. Gibson twenty-five years ago. After long search I found that the fragment, on which it was, had been turned face-up under a *nim* tree, and used as a seat by the idlers of the village, who had with their barbarous hinder parts obliterated the inscription (never very deep or clear cut) beyond all hope of transcription or estampage, though it is possible that a competent Sanskrit scholar, with time and the stone before him, might decipher a few words."

## RATANVĀDI

At the small village, of Ratanvādi, twenty miles further up the Pravarā valley from Akolā, is the almost complete old temple of Amriteśvara, measuring sixty-one feet by thirty feet. It is built upon very nearly the same plan as that of Siddheśvara at Akolā, and, like it, has a back entrance into the shrine. Instead of the porch-like wings to the hall, we find here shallow recesses in which are perforated windows. Possibly this was necessary as a precaution against the intrusion of wild beasts, as the temple is so close to the forests and defiles of the *ghāts*, the hamlet not being itself large enough to inspire fear and respect. (Plate LXX.)

The roof of the *maṇḍapa* has disappeared, leaving the inner lining or shell of the ceiling, but the *śikhara*, over the shrine, is almost entire, and is a very ornamental one. It is of the same style as that of Gondeśvara at Sinnar.

The walls are decorated in the same manner as those of the Akolā temple, but slightly varied in detail. There were no images on the walls of the temple excepting what were in the two niches, one on either side of the shrine outside.

The temple faces the west and is dedicated to Śiva, his *liṅga* being installed in the shrine. The Nandi, as at Akolā, is placed outside, facing the back door of the shrine.

## TAHĀKĀRI.

The temple of Bhavānī or Devī at Tahākāri, ten miles to the north-west of Akolā, is a three-shrined temple, in the principal shrine of which is an image of Mahālakshmī, whilst above the door is a *devī*. There are images in the three principal niches and the recesses around the shrine. The *śikharas* over

[1] Vol. V, page 8.

the shrines, which are very dilapidated, are built of brick like that of the temple at Kokamthān. The rest of the building, below the cornice, is of stone. Plates LXXI and (LXXIII—LXXV.)

The pillars, within the temple, are rather plain. In the central *maṇḍapa* which is common to all three shrines, there are twelve pillars in the square, namely, four principal corner ones and eight smaller, introduced as intermediate supports between them, as the span of beam is rather long between the corner pillars.

The ceiling of the *maṇḍapa* is particularly fine, it being most elaborately chiselled. It is almost hemispherical, and rises in the usual manner by concentric rings of cusped mouldings to the central pendant. The ceiling of the porch is also good. There are eight dancing bracket figures in the former, and there were six in the latter but two have disappeared.

There is an old Sanskrit inscription of *Saka* 1050 (A. D. 1128) on a pillar of the *maṇḍapa* of a small ruined shrine between this temple and the river.

## PEḌGĀON.

Pedgāon, eight miles south of Śrīgunda, stands in rather a commanding position on the high bank of the Bhimā. The village occupies a long strip of land which, with the river on the other side, hems in an old Musalmān enclosure which is roughly a quarter of a mile square, almost completely overrun with prickly pear. The fort is said to have been built by the Dakhan viceroy Khān Jahān who was in camp here during the monsoon of 1672 when in pursuit of Sivāji. He gave the place the name of Bahādurgadh which has not been retained. The Muḥammadan buildings which, judging from the great amount of debris, must have been very extensive, have almost entirely disappeared, the most complete being the Bībī Maḥall, occupying a delightful position upon the ramparts overlooking the river. But, although nearly three times the age of the Musalmān remains, and despite the devastating effect of the spoiler's hand, there still remain, within the precincts of the fort, the ruins of five old temples, one of which, that of Lakshmī-Nārāyaṇa, is a perfect little gem. Pedgāon must have been a place of importance long before the advent of the Muḥammadans, and, perhaps, this was due, in great measure, to its favourable position on the Bhimā. At this point the Sarasvatī river, upon which Śrīgunda stands, joins the Bhimā, the junction of rivers being generally considered more or less sacred places. (Plates LXXIV and LXXVI—LXXXIV.)

The temple of Lakshmī-Nārāyaṇa, measuring about 54 by 35 feet when complete, is most profusely decorated both within and without, and its outer walls are thickly covered with image sculpture, which has come in for a certain amount of delicate attention from Musalmān iconoclasts. It is a Vaishṇava temple, facing west, built upon a high part of the bank above the river. Its tower, now absent, was, probably, like many of this class, constructed in brickwork. The basement mouldings are crowded with little figures of horses, elephants and men; the *asvathara* or horse moulding, just above the elephants, being very rarely found in these temples. The walls, pillars and door frames are all richly wrought, but by no means so minutely as in the temple of Ambarnātha.

The pillars are of a different type to those at Ambarnātha and Balsāne, having a new feature introduced which is found in most of the mediæval temples of North Gujarāt, namely, the water pot and foliage element.[1] It occurs in the temples at Jodghā and Kokamthān already described. In this case, however, the waterpot is rather masked by an ornamental ribbing of lotus buds and stalks which are bound around it by a narrow band or fillet. The foliage, very much conventionalised, hangs over the lip of the jar or pot and forms four corners upon which rests a thin square slab.[2] The waterpot, with and without foliage, enters very largely into the designs of the pillars in the cave-temples, where, as in the Kārli cave, it forms, without foliage, the greater part of the base and, inverted, the capital of the pillar.

The large band of images, around the walls, is not cut with the same delicacy of touch as in the earlier work; but the figures stand out boldly from the walls and are very effective.

The hall, which had three porches, is enclosed by perforated screen walls, as may be seen in the elevation on Plate LXXXI, which allowed more light and air into the interior than in the older temples. This perforated panelling, like that in the side shrine at Kokamthān, is very plain when compared with the decoration of the shrine walls, and is an effective foil to the latter. Nor is it anything so rich as that found in Chālukyan temples, such as that of Trikuteśvara at Gadag in the Dhārwār District. It is here, perhaps, more the result of economy than any special purpose of design, for it is very evident that, for these later temples, not so much money was forthcoming as for the earlier. This, too, may account for the brick and plaster towers as found in the Kokamthān example.

In the photograph, Plate LXXVIII, is seen the rough method of laying the foundations of the building with rough boulders upon the ground surface, already noticed in the Architectural Note.

Standing out in front of this temple, and facing it, is the ruined temple of Bāleśvara. It is a picturesque pile of ruins, and looks particularly fine in the evening, backed up with the setting sun and the far-away windings of the Bhimā. Besides these, the other temples here are those of Rāmeśvara, Kholeśvara (called also Malikārjuna) and Bhairavnātha, originally a Jaina temple. There is nothing particularly striking about these. They are sadly ruined and dismantled, the shrine only, in each case, standing, the rest being heaps of ruins.

---

[1] See *The Architectural Antiquities of Northern Gujarāt*, by Dr. Jas. Burgess and Mr. H. Cousens.

[2] This carries out the same idea as in Corinthian capitals, where the upward growing foliage, meeting the under surface of the flat tile or abacus, curls back upon itself, and, in the Indian examples, hangs down in more pendent masses. Good examples of this, occurring in early work in the cave-temples, may be seen in the plates LVIII, LXIII, LXVI (ribbed somewhat like the Pedgāon pillars) and LXXXIV in the *Cave-temples of India* (Fergussen and Burgess).

## KARJAT.

Karjat is twenty-one miles east by south of Śrīgunda. The temple of Mahādeva, though old, is of no particular merit. On the front of the shrine of Malikārjuna, outside the north gate of the town, is a row of very indecent figures. The temple of Nāgeśvara or Nāgoba, across the stream from this, has a shrine whose floor is six feet below the floor of the hall, which is approached by a flight of steps, leading down to it, from inside the shrine doorway. The antechamber to the shrine is about two feet lower than the hall floor. (Plate LXXXV.)

## MĀNDUGĀON AND LIMPANGĀON.

The temples at these two places are fair examples of the later temples which may be more correctly called "Hemaḍpanti" than most of those already described, built subsequently to the middle of the thirteenth century. They are conspicuous by the absence of image sculpture on the outside of their walls, the decoration being confined to mouldings in string courses and geometrical designs. As already surmised, this may be due to want of funds for a more elaborate building, or to the presence of the Muḥammadans in the country, who were sworn enemies to all forms of idolatry. Images displayed openly upon the exterior would only excite their fanaticism and be an invitation to their iconoclastic tendencies. The Hindus were beginning to find that their idols were safer stowed away within their shrines.

FIG. 12.—Pillar in the temple at Limpangāon.

On either side of the main porch of the temple of Siddheśvara at Limpangāon is a large perforated screen wall which is neatly designed in imitation of cross bars, and slightly decorated. The building looks heavy and massive. The pillars of the hall are very well proportioned. The temple is, in every respect, a much better one than any of those at Śrīgunda. (Plates LXXXV—LXXXVII.)

## ŚRĪGUNDA.

The temples of Vitobā, Rakhamāi, Hatkeśvara and Mahālakshmī, though old, are very plain and uninteresting structures. They are examples of a decadent class which is very widespread, and probably built when funds were not available to erect them in the more ornate style. The walls are perfectly plain and the only sculpture about them is poor, it being principally confined to the pillars and door frames. (Plate LXXXVI.)

Some very good wood-carving decorates the façades of two houses at Śrīgunda, of the style, though not so old, as that found in such abundance in many of the old towns of North Gujarāt.[1] It is very similar to that upon some of the old Marāthā palaces in the city of Poona, and that which was brought from Kittur, in the Dhārwār District, when the Desāi's palace was demolished in the insurrection of 1824, of which a beautifully carved doorway was preserved in the local Magistrate's office at Hubli. In plate LXXXVI the brackets remind one much of those, in stone, under the cornices of the old mosques and tombs at Bijāpur. The application of the decoration on the door frames is particularly well carried out. The blank square in the middle of the lower lintel probably had a painted picture of Gaṇapati or some other favourite deity.

---

[1] See *The Architectural Antiquities of North Gujarāt*, by Dr. Jas. Burgess. C.I.E., and Henry Cousens, Plates IV, XX, XXI, XXII, XXXVI and XLVI.

# TEMPLES IN THE SĀTĀRĀ DISTRICT.

## KHATĀV.

THE Sātārā District has a very poor lot of old temples. At Katāv, some twenty-five miles east of Sātārā, are a few old examples of the "Hemadpanti" class, the most complete among them being that of Nāganātha across the stream bed upon the north-west of the town. It occupies a conspicuous position upon high ground, having an open front with a neatly decorated façade. It is a small building, measuring no more than 60 by 30 feet, and consists of a plain square hall, antechamber and shrine. Four pillars support the central ceiling, and two more the eaves and cornice of the open front. The pillars are of the later Chālukyan type. Gaṇapati presides above the shrine doorway, and, within, is the *liṅga*. The *śikhara*, or spire, has disappeared. Without, facing the shrine, is the bull Nandi. (Plates LXXXVIII and LXXXIX.)

Beside this temple is a smaller one of Gaṇapati, which, having been stripped of the outer casing of its walls, shows the manner of building, and the rough backs of the blocks forming the inner shell.

The temple of Someśvara, in the fields beyond the stream, on the north of the town, is similar to that of Nāganātha, but smaller. It was never finished, much of its decoration being merely traced out on the walls. The temple of Bhāiroba, in the village, is a long clumsily-built old shrine, on either side of the entrance doorway of which stands a roughly carved *viragal*. The temple of Nārāyaṇadeva, near by, consists of a partly ruined old temple repaired and added to with brick and mortar masonry, and a wooden-tiled *maṇḍapa* or hall. Nārāyaṇadeva is set up within the shrine, but, in a niche in the inner hall, is placed a *liṅga*. There is rather a good doorway inserted in the entrance to the courtyard.

## KĀTARKHATĀV.

At Kātarkhatāv, twelve miles south-east of Khatāv, is the old temple of Kātareśvara of similar construction to that at Khatāv. The pillars are better finished. Along the face of the façade wall are several indecent figures in panels. The temple has portions of its original brick tower remaining, sufficient to show that it rose after the Chālukyan style, with cusped arches, as in the temple of Kāsiviśveśvara at Lakkuṇḍi, the brickwork having had a thin layer of plaster over it. Where a part of the walls has fallen away at the back, may be seen the mode of "filling-in", between the outer and the inner casings, with boulders eight to ten inches in diameter set in a grouting of white mud. (Plates LXXXIX and XC.)

## GURSĀLA.

The temples of Gursāla, a few miles to the south-west of Kātarkhatāv, are of special interest. That of Somaliṅga, in the village, has its spire intact. The total disappearance of the spires of the great majority of the old Chālukyan and "Hemaḍpanti" temples seems almost unaccountable. The finely-carved stone spires of those that are left would lead one to suppose that they were all in that material. But this shrine, the Kātarkhatāv one, and a few to be found in the adjoining Haidarābād territory, shew that brick spires were in as much, if not greater, use than those of stone, but whether on account of the greater lightness of the mass or the cheaper mode of construction, it is difficult to say. This temple of Somaliṅga is a very solidly built structure, whose walls are severely plain. The pillars, within, are also plain, but are well proportioned. (Plates XC—XCIII.)

The temple of Rāmaliṅga, outside the village, is a neat little combination of *kuṇḍa*, or tank, and shrine, the latter standing upon the west margin of the tank, and forming, with it, part of one general design. There is a row of the usual grossly indecent figures on the front wall of the temple. The tank is square, with flights of steps leading down to the water's edge from an inside platform which runs around some distance below ground level, the stair to which descends from the side opposite the temple.

## SIṄGHAṆĀPUR.

Siṅghaṇāpur, with its celebrated temple and fine large tank, is situated in a depression in the hills upon the very crest of the high tableland which here falls abruptly into the valley of the Nīrā, about forty miles to the east by north of Sātārā. From the hills around, and especially from the court of the great temple, which is perched upon the highest summit, a magnificent view of the country below is obtained, which stretches away from Phaltan to Mālsiras and further. The town is said to have been founded by the Yādava king Siṅghaṇa (A. D. 1210-1247), who is also credited with having built one hundred temples of Śiva daily! (Plates XCI, XCII and XCIV.)

The great temple of Śambhu Mahādeva, which is a good example of a very late "Hemaḍpanti" temple, is situated about three quarters of a mile west of the village upon the highest point of the range, and is a conspicuous object for miles around. Beneath this temple, upon the north side, is the older one of Amriteśvara, while, around them both, upon the sloping eastern and northern sides of the hill, nestles the little village of Brahman ministrants. A broad flight of steps leads down, under two great archways, to the plain beneath, where it joins the road which connects the hill with the village. On either side of this road are *dharmaśālas* or rest-houses, wells, and *samāds* or tombs.

The present temple of Śambhu Mahādeva is a reconstruction of an older one, or, rather, a new building entirely erected upon the site of an older, the pillars, lintels and other fragments of which lie about the hill. The present temple is said to have been built by the great Marātha chief Śivāji (1627-1680). In the Nandi pavilion, hanging from the roof, are two old bells dated 1720, in Roman letters, which probably belonged to some old Portuguese church in the Konkaṇ. The columns are copied from those of the older building, but the work is not quite so good. The lower temple of Amriteśvara, which is said to have been in existence before the larger one, is probably coeval with the foundation of the town. It is now in a very shattered condition, and is dangerously unsafe for use, nevertheless people use it, and stand about unconcernedly under tons of cracked masses of stone whose temporary props look as if they might collapse at any moment.

Near by are the tombs of Shāhji, the father, and of Śambhaji, the son, of Śivāji. The great tank is ascribed to Māloji, the grandfather of Śivāji.

# TEMPLES IN THE SHOLĀPUR DISTRICT.

## MĀLSIRAS.

THE Sholāpur District is even more bare of antiquarian remains than the Sātārā District, and, what there is, is not of very much account. At Mālsiras, fifty miles west by north from Sholāpur, are the ruins of two old temples—that of Someśvara, just inside the north-east gate of the town, and that of Mahābaleśvara, a short distance outside to the north-east, on the bank of the stream. The former stands upon a high basement and is much ruined—the shrine, without its tower, and some of the pillars and beams of the *maṇḍapa* alone standing. Carved blocks for the ceiling lie about, and the temple, generally, looks as if it had been left unfinished. The other shrine is rather a mean little building, but, though old, it is in a better state of preservation than the first. (Plate XCV.)

## VELĀPUR.

Ten miles south-east of Mālsiras is the village of Velāpur, where, by the roadside, just outside the village, is a plain, but well-preserved old stone temple with a well-built *dharmaśāla,* or rest-house, beside it. Around the temple, set up in the ground, were about twenty well-carved *viragals* or hero stones. One of these was sent away in order to be placed in the Prince of Wales Museum in Bombay. There were seven in one line, and the rest were scattered about. The sculptures upon them represent battle scenes in which the heroes distinguish and extinguish themselves, the same heroes in paradise, and the worship of the *liṅga.* They are not so delicately and minutely carved as many that are found in the Kanarese districts where the Chālukyan style of architecture prevails, but are much the same in other respects. *Viragals* are not often found in the Dakhan, *satī* stones, commemorating the self-immolation of widows, being more common. One small one would seem to indicate that the deceased met his death in the chase. Another stone bears a representation of Gaja-Lakshmī, or Lakshmī with her elephants pouring water over her. (Plate XCIII, XCV—XCVII.)

Upon the far side of the adjacent tank is another double-shrined old temple of the "Hemaḍpanti" class. In the village is the temple of Hara-

Hareśvara which is a conglomeration of buildings, the nucleus of which is a triple-shrined old temple of poor construction. At the side of the steps, leading down to a square tank in front of it, is an inscription which records the setting up of a *kalaśa* or finial, or, in other words the consecration and dedication of a temple by Brahmādevarāna, a subordinate chief under the king Praudhapratapachavartin Śri Rāmchandradeva in *śaka* 1227 (A. D. 1305). Another, partly abraided inscription, on a rough block of stone near the entrance to the temple, records a gift of lands by the chief Johādeva in Samvat 1922, during the same king's reign

FIG. 13—Pillars in the temple of Velāpur.

## PAṆḌHARPUR.

Before leaving the Sholāpur District we may notice the celebrated temple of Viṭhobā at Paṇḍharpur, on the banks of the Bhimā. Though of little interest from an architectural point of view, this Vaishṇava shrine is of vast importance in the eyes of the people of this side of India. Four times a year, but more especially on two of these occasions, pilgrims from far and near congregate in thousands, arriving, with their pilgrim staves and banners, and the tinkling of bells, by train, bullock cart, on foot or pony-back, weary and footsore. Some even come upon all fours, measuring their length in dots and dashes along the whole journey, among whom not a few artfully mark out the forward limit of each stretch with a short cane or stick thus gaining a foot or more upon each length. On arrival at Paṇḍharpur they at once fall willing victims to the wily priests, who discover their family names in their respective lists, and appropriate them accordingly. These constitute themselves their spiritual and mundane ministrants for the period of their stay in the town, which is generally limited by the amount of ready cash the devotee possesses, or rather the amount he can be induced to part with. Having bathed in the river and shaved off his moustache, if he possesses one, the pilgrim is taken to make his first call upon Viṭhobā and Rakhamāī Devī, and the minor deities who patiently await him in the many smaller shrines surrounding the main one. Here he obtains absolution, and various other favours and privileges, according to the weight of his purse, for Viṭhobā is a respector of persons. The open-handed pilgrim he receives in his best clothes and jewels, and the more of the latter are piled on the more that open hand contains.

Viṭhobā is said to have come originally from Dwārkā on a visit to a certain youth Puṇḍalika who constrained the god to take up his abode at Paṇḍharpur. How he came, or the date of his coming, no man knows: these are idle questions; he came and that is enough. But though we cannot tell when he came, we can make a shrewd guess as to when he was housed in his present temple. It is a more or less recent structure, but there are remains of older temples about the town, and evidence that this particular one has been in part built from the materials of a more ancient shrine; but whether it stood on the site of the present one it is hard to say. That the present temple succeeded an older one to the same deity there can be little doubt, for an inscription upon a pilaster of a former temple, now used as an over-head beam in the present, tells us, in Kanarese and Sanskrit, that the Hopsāla king Vira-Someśvara, in *Samvat*, 1159 (A. D. 1237), gave a gift of gold to the god Viṭṭhala, which is an older form of the name Viṭhobā. Portions of this inscription, in its present position, are covered by the overlapping of the capitals of the pillars below it, thus shewing that it could not have been engraved in its present position. Between the present temple and the river is a portion of an old temple converted into a *chāvadi* or police station. The pillars are all standing in their original positions, and upon one of them is an inscription in Sanskrit verse recording the fact that a subordinate chief Kesavamaṇḍalika performed the *aptoryama* sacrifice in the temple of Paṇḍu-ranga Viṭṭhala on the banks of the Bhimarathī in *Samvat* 1192 (A. D. 1270). This would make it appear that this was the original temple of Viṭhobā. Between this, again, and the river, are the remains of two other small shrines. The present temple of Viṭhobā, which is shut in upon all sides with houses has been built in instalments, the *śikhara* or spire having been erected within the last sixty years; the substructure might go back two hundred years, hardly more.

## VANGI AND WARKUT.

At the villages of Vangi and Warkut are a few odd remains but they are not of much consequence. At the former place are the ruins of some small old shrines; at the latter, a number of old sculptures which formed part of an old temple now no more. They represent Vishṇu and Śiva in different forms, Indra with his elephant, and a Diana of the chase. (Plate XCVIII.)

# TEMPLES IN BERAR.

## BĀRSI TĀKLI.

THE few Hindu remains in Berār may be included in the temples of the Dakhan, since they are well within the limits of the Dakhan as the term was understood in mediæval times, and are of the same nature and style as those to be found further west. It is only, however, in the southern districts of the province that they are found in any numbers, the northern districts being remarkably bare of remains.

On the outskirts of the town of Bārsi Tākli, twelve miles to the south-east of Akolā, the famous cotton centre, is the compact little black-stone temple of Bhavānī. It consists of a *maṇḍapa* and shrine, both being freely decorated upon the exterior with bands of mouldings and images. The *maṇḍapa* is curiously arranged with regard to the shrine, being attached, as it were, side-

Fig. 14—Pillar in Kālikā Devi's temple.

ways to it, or, in other words, the hall may be described as having its entrance on one side instead of at the end opposite the shrine as is usual. The entrance to the hall is thus at right-angles to that of the shrine. The plan of the hall is rectangular while that of the shrine is star-shaped, which is carried out in the plans of the four decorated pillars which support the central ceiling. A broad band of images runs round the outer walls, the principal ones in which, excepting Gaṇapati, being females. Mahākālī and Mahiśāsuramardanī occupying important positions. This is what might be expected in a temple dedicated to a *devī* or goddess, and shows that Bhavānī is not a recent installation in the shrine. The walls are not free from indecent representations. The ceiling is particularly well decorated, the marginal panels being very much like those of temple No. 1 at Balsāne in Khāndesh. The *śikhara* of the shrine and the roof of the hall have disappeared. (Plates XCIX—CI.)

Within the temple, engraved upon the back wall, is a long Sanskrit inscription which is, unfortunately, very much damaged by the peeling of the surface of the stone. It is dated in *Śaka* 1098 (A. D. 1176), which, from the style of the temple, may be taken as about the date of its construction.

There is a second temple at Bārsi Tākli, that of Śrī Koleśvara Mahādeva, of comparatively late work, in the debased mixed Muḥammadan style. Its interior is much below ground level and is always full of water, which percolates through from the adjacent rivulet.

## ŚIRPUR.

Śirpur is twelve miles west by north of Bāsim. A short distance outside the village, on the west, stands the old temple of Antariksha Pārśvanātha belonging to the Digambara Jaina community. At present, their principal temple is a very modern one in the village, but the other was the original one from which, according to tradition, the image was transferred, probably about the time of the Muḥammadan invasion of the country. In the new temple they have the usual underground chambers in which to conceal their images in the event of a repetition of the treatment they once received at the hands of those iconoclasts. The old temple has an abraided inscription which seems to read *Saṁvat* 1334 (A. D. 1412), and the name Antariksha Pārśvanātha. The plan of the shrine is star-shaped, and the walls are decorated with bands of arabesque, no images being present except what were in the three principal niches. The temple gives one the impression of being unfinished, and it was probably erected quite a hundred years before the date of the inscription. Its erection was possibly interrupted during the early incursions of the Muḥammadans into the Dakhan. The hybrid style of *śikhara*, which was commenced, but left unfinished, is manifestly later than the stone sculptured walls. It is of brick and mortar. The entrance doorway of the hall is elaborately carved and has images at the bottom on either side; but these would have been more or less hidden from outside observation by the covering porch when completed. Among these are nude Jaina figures, and above the lintel, upon the dedicatory block is a small seated Jina. There are now, in the shrine, two small marble

Jinas, but neither of them is Pārśvanātha. They are much neglected and receive little attention. (Plate CII.)

## MEHKAR.

Mehkar is about forty-five miles to the south-east of Buldāna. At the north-west corner of the town, overlooking the river, and enclosed within a mud-walled enclosure, is a partly ruined old *dharmaśālā* or travellers' rest-house, which, in the past, has been badly used. Much of the building has fallen since it was photographed by Major Gill over fifty years ago, and many of its pillar shafts are scattered about the town, several being near the market place. This *dharmaśālā* was, perhaps, a subsidiary building to an important temple, possibly Jaina, which stood near and above it, but which has now disappeared. The foundation or retaining walls of the site upon which the temple stood can be seen running round the *dharmaśālā*, and from it right up to the town gate, a little way to the east of it. At first sight, the wall here looks like a portion of the town wall, but it is not so, though it may have done duty for such in later times. A town wall would not have a series of horizontal offsets forming ledges all the way up its outer side, by which an enemy could easily climb up. Moreover the wall is of the Hindu period, while the present gate is of the Muḥammadan. (Plate CIII and CIX.)

The *dharmaśālā* is about 72 feet square inside, and is formed by a deep covered colonnade, with two rows of pillars, surrounding a small central square courtyard 23 feet square, which is open to the sky, and whose pavement is sunk a few feet below the floor of the colonnade. There were sixty pillars in all, of which twenty-five still stand. The central courtyard has been filled up with earth to bring it to a level with the rest. All the pillars around the north and east side of the court, with the enclosing wall, have gone, but many of their bases still remain. There is a marked absence of figure sculpture upon the building, the decoration on the pillars being almost entirely confined to geometric and conventional leaf designs. The building is of a comparatively late date.

There is a new temple of Bālāji, higher up in the town, which was built not many years ago, to enshrine a finely carved blackstone image of Vishṇu which was dug up close by. The image is full life-size, and is now enveloped in tawdry petticoats, but does not seem to be very old notwithstanding its elaborate detail. At the same time were found a quantity of old corroded and fragmentary copper-plate grants. Among the loose sculptured stones lying near the temple is the lower part of the body of a life-sized seated Jina, while inside Bālāji's temple is a broken Jaina image with the date *Saṁvat* 1272 (A. D. 1350) upon it in a short inscription.

## LOṆĀR.

One of the best remaining examples in Berār of these old mediæval temples is that at Loṇār in the south-east corner of the Buldāna District, known as the temple of Daitya-Sūdana. It is a Vaishṇava shrine and receives its name from its connection with the story of the demon Lavaṇāsura or Loṇāsura who used to dwell in the crater close by, and who was eventually slain by Vishṇu in his incarnation of Daitya-Sūdana. The temple measures 105 feet long by 84½ feet broad. It faces east, and is built of black stone, profusely carved all over the exterior with images and other ornament. The work, however, is comparatively late as may be seen in the inferior workmanship of the images, the style of mouldings, particularly those in the basement, and the indiscriminate spreading of ornament over every available surface. The building seems never to have been finished, the roof and some parts of the top of the walls with the top of the three doorways of the hall, not having been completed. There is a total absence of sculptured stone lying about, and some fragments would surely have remained had the building been finished and subsequently ruined. The four principal pillars, that would have supported the dome of the hall, together with part of the inside masonry lining of the walls, were never erected; but, at a very much later date, the building was again taken in hand and finished off in a rough and ready manner, with coarse brickwork, and brick arching was thrown over the unfinished tops of the three doorways. The moulded basements for the porches before the doorways were laid, but the porches were not put up. The work was probably cut short by the inroads of the Muḥammadans about the end of the thirteenth or beginning of the fourteenth century. When the temple was again taken in hand and the brickwork was added, a modern and very poor image of Vishṇu, said to have been brought from Nāgpur at great cost, was set up in the shrine, and this is now the object of worship. The plan of both the hall and shrine is star-shaped. (Plates CI and CIII.)

Occupying the principal niche on the back of the temple, outside, is a standing image of Sūrya; and, as this is the position of the leading image on the exterior, and usually has direct connection with the image in the shrine, it is just possible that the temple may have been intended as a temple to Sūrya. Of the other two principal niches, that on the south has an image of a *devī*, but which one it is impossible to say, owing to its mutilated state. The north niche is empty. One of the side shrines of the modern temple at the head of the descent into the crater, close by, near the tank and *gaumukha*, contains some old loose images of Sūrya and Narasiṁha which may have come from this temple.

The three niches mentioned are very prominent features, inasmuch as they project like miniature porches, a deep heavy cornice, supported upon two forward pillarettes, protecting them. The basement, with its lines of mouldings projecting like great square buttresses, supports them. Among the images on the exterior are Vishṇu, Narasiṁhā, Varāha, Gaṇapati, Brahmā, Bhairava, Sarasvatī, Paraśurāma, Rāma, Kaliya-mardanī and the Regents of the eight points of the compass in their respective positions.

Out in front of the temple, at a short distance from the main entrance, is the basement of a pavilion, but the upper portion of it was never built. When the later brickwork was added to the main building, a square mass was built here with a niche on each of its four sides. In that facing the temple was placed a rough image of Garuḍa, the *vāhana* of Vishṇu. One or two small pillars stand in the courtyard, which were, perhaps, intended for this pavilion or the temple porches.

In the south-east corner of the courtyard of the temple is a small plain temple facing the north. Its exterior is built in with mud walls. Within it are three old images brought from elsewhere, the principal one of which is of Vishṇu, supported upon one side by Brahmā.

At a short distance to the west of the town is an old *dharmaśālā*, or travellers' rest-house, composed of corridors of cut-stone pillars. It is in rather a dilapidated condition.

## LONĀR CRATER AND ITS TEMPLES.

At a short distance to the west of the town is what is supposed to be the crater of an extinct volcano, the only one known in the Dakhan. It is a great bowl-shaped hollow, five miles around at the top, and about three miles five hundred feet below, where a salt lake occupies the centre, surrounded by a wide margin of land between the bottom of the slope and the edge of the lake. The inner walls of the crater, which differ in nothing from ordinary hill-side covered with jungle and grass, slope down from the upper rim at an abrupt angle of 75° to 80° to the level belt around the lake. In the outer ring of this belt tamarind trees and date palms thrive, while the inner, nearest the lake, supports the bābul tree only. On the northern margin of the lake, where this belt of land is widest, are kitchen gardens and fruit trees watered by the stream which descends from the *gaumukha* above. The water of the lake is impregnated with a salt which is extracted and sold as a marketable article for use in washing and dying cloth. Although the water is so saturated with this salt, which causes it to give off a very offensive smell, yet in a well, sunk quite close to its edge on the south side, the water is perfectly fresh and is used for drinking purposes.

Down in the bottom of the crater, around the margin of the lake, are a number of old temples, and there are others in the descent to the lake from the *gaumukha* temple. From this temple, down to the lake, extends a ravine which is the only break in the continuity of the circular walls of the crater, and it is down the sides of this cleft that the pathway leads to the bottom. The head of the ravine bifurcates near the top, and it is at the head of the western branch that the spring is located from which the water is led through a *gaumukha*, or cow's mouth, cut in stone, into a small square tank in which Hindu pilgrims of both sexes, old and young, bathe promiscuously. The water is supposed to come from the Ganges, in proof of which it is said that a marked stick thrown into that river was found to emerge at the spring! A temple, and an accumulation of small cell-shrines, all of more or less modern growth, have sprung up around the tank. The Muhammadans had the audacity to invade this snuggery of the Hindus, and they actually began to build a mosque right in their midst, upon the western side of the sacred tank, but were eventually stopped in their rash venture and were warned off. The foundation of the building still remains.

As most of the temples in the crater are in disuse, and have lost their names, I have numbered them, starting with this group as No. 1. About a third of the way down, standing upon the point of a spur between the two branches of the ravine, is another Śaiva temple, No. 2, partly rebuilt, but of no special interest. A short distance below this, on a low knoll, is the site of another temple, but the building has disappeared.

Beyond the last temple is No. 3, the most ornate of all. It stands at the bottom of the ravine on the outer edge of the gardens. It faces west, and consists of an open pillared *maṇḍapa* and shrine, but is in a sadly dilapidated condition, and the shrine is in ruins. The *maṇḍapa* had three porches. When intact it must have been as pretty a temple as any in the neighbourhood.

On the north margin of the lake, the gardens separating it from it, is No. 4. It is similar to Nos. 5 and 6, and is in ruins. It faces east and has a *liṅga* in the shrine.

No. 5 is a small plain temple to the north-west of the lake. It consists of a shrine and *maṇḍapa*, the outer walls being built in the plain block-in-course of the late "Hemāḍpanti" style, but it is much ruined. Beside it are the ruins of a small square cistern.

No. 6, a little further round towards the west, is a facsimile of the last, even to its ruinous state, and like it, it faces the east. The lower portion of the walls and the whole surface of the pillars are much weatherworn and corroded, but the beams, which are protected by the roof, are sharp and clean. The temple measures 40 by 20 feet, roughly. The roofing seems to have been of concrete and brickwork.

Almost due west of the lake is No. 7. It is of the same style as the last two, but almost twice as large and equally ruined. The temple faces east and has a *liṅga* in the shrine. During a late famine one or two rough pits were dug near by for water, which now contain a quantity, so foul-smelling and stagnant, that it is almost impossible to stand within fifty yards of them. This is probably due to the salt in the water that has percolated through from the lake, and which is supposed to be the blood and decomposed flesh of the giant Lavaṇāsura who was slain and buried in this den of his. The smell is strong corroboration of the story! Around the temple is a fine grove of banyan, tamarind, and custard apple trees, and palm tree stumps.

No. 9 is the more modern temple of Bhavānī Devī, which is due south of the lake and faces the north as most Devī temples do, such as that at Bārsi Tākli. It consists of a shrine and *maṇḍapa* with three doorways, and is conspicuous from afar by its coat of whitewash. In front of the main entrance is a small *yoni-kuṇḍa*, but the shape of the fire-pit, instead of being that of the *yoni*, is perfectly heart-shaped, with its point towards the east. Just behind the temple is a very small one, No. 8, in ruins, in which is a *liṅga*.

Temple No. 10 is on the south-east margin of the lake, and is much like Nos. 5 and 6, but not quite so much ruined, and is a trifle larger It faces the east. The roof of the *maṇḍapa* has been covered with concrete and brickwork in which an abundance of broken rock crystal has been used. The pillars are of the same pattern as those of the *dharmaśalā* at Mehkar.

About two hundred yards further on from the last is No. 11, a temple about as large as No. 7. It faces the north, and consists of a shrine with three porches, two of which are in ruins. Against the back wall of the shrine is a seat or throne for an image which is absent. It is possible that this was a *devī's* temple and it may have been the one that preceded the later one now in use, No. 9. The outer walls of the shrine are plain, in late "Hemāḍpanti" style, being in block-in-course with simple broad projecting bands.

Temples Nos. 12 and 13, together with a square *kuṇḍa*, form a group a little way up the hillside on the east of the lake. The two temples face the west, No. 12 being a Vaishṇava temple. It consists of a shrine and *maṇḍapa* with three porches, and is in a fairly good state of repair. The *maṇḍapa*, which was open all around, has been closed up with rough walling between the pillars. Above the shrine doorway is Garuḍa, and in the shrine is the ruined altar for an image. The pillars of the hall are much like those at Mehkar, plainly blocked out but without ornament. Upon the side of the west doorway is inscribed the name Vāsugī, which is the same name found upon the Mehkar building, and is, perhaps, that of a mason.

Temple No. 13 is slightly to the back and north of the last and is a Śaiva shrine in ruins. It has three porches, and the pillars are like those at Mehkar. In front of this, and to the side of No. 12, is a well built *kuṇḍa* or reservoir.

No. 14 is situated between the last and the lake, and is about the same size as Nos. 5 and 6. The exterior is plain, but the shrine is star-shaped in plan. The pillared *maṇḍapa* is in ruins, the pillars being slightly more ornate than at Mehkar. The temple faces the north and the shrine is half filled with earth.

Still nearer to the margin of the lake is the site of temple No. 15.

This completes the ring of temples around the lake in the bottom of the crater. Ascending, again, by the same ravine, but taking the eastern branch at the top, we come to the ruins of a small temple, No. 16. It faces the east and consists of a shrine, the remains of a pavilion in front of it, and a *kuṇḍa* beside it. It has plain undecorated walls, but the shrine door-frame is particularly well carved. The pavilion is supported upon four well-carved pillars which look like earlier work than anything else at the lake; and the ceiling is also well decorated with cusped ornament of the style of the work found in Tejahpāla's temple at Mt. Ābu. The outer part of the roof has fallen.

## SĀTGĀON.

At Sātgāon, four miles to the north by west of Chikhli in the Buldānā District, there is a rather fine old temple of Vishṇu. It faces the west. In the shrine, against the back wall, is a seat, or throne, in three tiers. In the centre of the face of the upper is Garuḍa, and in the centre of the middle one is a *devī* or goddess. Standing upright upon the seat is a slotted stone intended to hold a standing image, a small fragment of which, with the feet only, is in position, the rest being destroyed. The ceilings of the *maṇḍapa* are very well decorated, and, in style, seem to stand half way between the later temples of the 13th and 14th centuries and those of the 11th. The pillars, too, are of an intermediate type. The *maṇḍapa* is in a very shattered condition, many of the pillars being canted over at very dangerous angles and threatening to collapse. The exterior walls of the shrine are decorated with the usual basement mouldings, which are surmounted by bands and panels of arabesque in place of images, excepting for the three empty niches which held loose ones. A portion of the *śikhara* stands, and it rises in the style of that of Gondeśvara at Sinnar, which it closely resembles. There are small niches and images around the base of the *śikhara* and on the *maṇḍapa* roof. The dwarf wall around the *maṇḍapa* is decorated, on the outside, with little pilasters and images alternately. There are brackets, half way up the shafts of the pillars of the porches, which, it is clear, were adorned, as at Gondeśvara, with bracket images. (Plates CVI—CIX.)

Beside this temple, on the north, is a smaller one which is now a wreck. A photograph taken about fifty years ago shows that very much more was then standing.

At a short distance to the east of the larger temple and between it and the village, is a portion of an old building which, with the addition of some mud walls, has been converted into a temple by the villagers, and a *liṅga* has been placed within it. The building looks like the gateway and porch of an enclosure that once went round the big temple and its subsidiary buildings. A seat ran round the inside porch, where the Nandi now is, and within the doorway was an open hall with a seat around the sides. The doorway is elaborately carved, and has the usual Gaṇeśa on the dedicatory block. Above this, in a row of niches, are Vaishṇavī, Brahmī, and Pārvatī in a row, Brahmī occupying the centre. As in the big temple, there are no male deities upon the doorway save Gaṇeśa; they are all *devīs*. Nor are there any images on either side at the bottom, or upon that of the shrine of the main temple; the latter, too, has no images above the cornice over Gaṇeśa, the usual place for them being taken up by a band of lozenge-shaped ornament. Round the beams of the central dome of the main temple there is nothing but a row of *devīs* with attendants, and the only images on the main pillars of the hall are four small ones on each base, one on each side, all being *devīs*.

A little way to the north of the large temple are four standing pillars, all that remain of a small temple. A short distance to the north-west of this is a large *pippala* tree with a high platform around it, on which are some fragments of old images. Among them is the lower portion of an image of Pārśvanātha with an inscription of two lines beneath dated *Śaka* 1173 (A.D. 1251). It is Digambara, its nakedness being distinctly indicated. Another image, that of a *devī*, is in two pieces—the bust, and the legs with the seat. She is two-armed, has necklaces and earrings, and her hair is done up in a big chignon at the back. The left hand rests upon the knee and holds a fruit; the right hand has gone. Above her head is a wreath of flowers, over which is seated a little Jina, and beneath her seat are three panels, in the centre one of which are three heads in a row, each with a pyramidal coiled head-dress. Under the *devī's* left knee is a small tiger or lion. It is probably intended to represent Ambikā (Ambājī, Ambādevī or Ambā Bhavānī), a favourite Jaina goddess.

FIG. 15.—A broken image at Sātgāon.

## SĀKEGĀON.

Another temple of the same style and age as that at Sātgāon, and in an equally ruinous state, is that of Mahādeva at the village of Sākegāon, six miles west of Chikhli. It faces the east, and consists of a shrine, an antechamber and a hall, with a porch in front of the entrance on the east. It was surrounded by a heavily-built wall enclosing a courtyard, the entrance to which is on the north side. To the south of the main building is a small subsidiary temple facing the north, against which the surrounding wall abuts on either side, from which it is evident that the wall was built after the shrine. The masonry of the walls, and the pillars of the courtyard gateway, are of the same style and age as those of the temple at Mehkar, and therefore later than the temple itself. (Plate CX.)

The walls of the *maṇḍapa* and shrine are quite free of images, save for those in two of the three large niches round the shrine, and are decorated with the usual basement mouldings and bands of geometric ornament. The back wall of the shrine, or rather its outer casing, has fallen, carrying with it a great part of the spire on that side. The back niche has gone with it. In the niche on the south side is an image of Nateśa, or the *tāṇḍava* of Śiva, and in that on the north side is an image of Mahākālī. The front of the tower is decorated with the trifoliated *chaitya* arch, and, under it, are the images of the *tāṇḍava* and of Śiva and Pārvatī, while upon the sides of the same are those of Bhairava, Mahiśāsura-mardanī and Gaṇapati. Within the shrine is the *liṅga*.

In the small temple, on the south side of the main building, against the back wall, is a seat for an image, but it is now absent, and it is not known to what deity the shrine was dedicated.

## KOTHALI.

At Kothali, twelve miles south-east of Pīmpalgāon-Rājā in the Buldānā District, are two old temples of the "Hemāḍpanti" class. The largest the temple of Mahādeva—is in the town, and has three shrines with one common hall. It faces the east and has Gaṇeśa over the shrine doorways, all of which are elaborately carved. In the main shrine is an old square *śālunka* with a circular hole for a *liṅga*; but the latter has gone. In the side shrine, on the north, is a *liṅga*, but the shrine on the south is empty. The hall has no pillars. The porch before the entrance has fallen, the platform, only, remaining. Out in front of this porch stand the ruins of what was once, perhaps, the Nandi pavilion, but it is ruined. Beyond this, again, are the remains of the main entrance to the temple courtyard with its steps. The *śikhara* was probably built of brickwork, since some brick masonry remains upon the roof and no carved *śikhara* stones lie about. (Plate CXI.)

The second temple is outside the village to the south-east. It is dedicated to Chintāmaṇi, and faces west. It is made up of a shrine and *maṇḍapa*, the latter being supported upon four pillars. Gaṇeśa presides upon the lintel. The shrine doorway is carved, but not so elaborately as in the first temple.

## DHOTRA.

At Dhotra, eighteen miles south of Chikhli, are three old temples, the one about a quarter of a mile south of the village, in the fields, being the most important. It is a temple of Śiva, faces the east, and consists of a shrine and a closed *maṇḍapa*. The entrance is in the east end of the hall, opposite the shrine, while, off each of the two sides of the hall, is a deep recess like a shallow shrine without a doorway. A most unusual thing with the pilasters in this temple is that their shafts are built in sections, with the courses of the wall masonry, and are not, as in earlier work, a single stone built into the wall. The bracket capitals of the pillars have the cobra ornament upon them. Within the shrine is a *liṅga*. The dedicatory blocks above the shrine doorways have been left plain without images. (Plate CXII.)

FIG. 16.—Pillar in the old temple at Dhotra.

The exterior of the temple is fully moulded in horizontal bands of mouldings running round the whole of the walls, but there are no images, not even those three principal ones usually found upon the walls of the shrine. In this, as well as in temple No. 11 at Lonar, we find bands of chequered squares used in the ornament. That is, the surface of the stone is marked out into one inch squares, every alternate one being sunk. This was a favourite, and often characteristic ornament in very early temples, such as those of the Gupta period, but seems to have fallen out of use, in Western India at least, and not to have been used again until resuscitated in these very late shrines.

On the west of the village is another old temple, but it is very much dilapidated. It has a shrine and hall with a porch and entrance on the east The whole of the *maṇḍapa* has fallen with the roofing of the porch. The exterior is severely plain.

On the north-west of the village is another old ruined shrine with a closed *maṇḍapa,* from which the outer casing of the walls has gone. The shrine is empty; the temple faces the east. In a row, over the shrine door, are nine faces, the third from each end having a curved tusk in the two corners of the mouth, otherwise the faces are alike.

# TEMPLE IN H. E. H. THE NIZAM'S TERRITORY.

## AUNDHA.

At Aundha, some forty miles to the south of Bāsim, in Haidarābād territory, is one of the twelve famous *jyotirlingas* of India in the temple of Nāgnātha. The town is of some importance and considerable trade, standing, as it does, at the crossing of the trade routes from Nirmal and the Śirpur forests to Jālna and Aurangābād, and from Haidarābād to the Berārs. A very heavily-built stone wall originally surrounded the town, portions of which still exist. It is very pleasantly situated in a level and well cultivated plain surrounded by an amphitheatre of hills. Upon the east and south it is approached by rather steep and rough passes which ascend from the lower country on those sides. It has the appearance of being an ancient place, for parts of very old walls still exist, which are far older than the crumbling ones which now partly surround the town. Ancient Jaina temples, as well as Hindu ones, once flourished here, their remains now being the foul-smelling abodes of the bat and owl.

The temple of Nāgānatha is a building of two periods, the older portions of which, from the ground level to the eaves, being probably thirteenth century work carried out in the style of the Hindu work of North Gujarāt of the same period. When compared with the work of the temple of Ambarnātha, it is seen to be not quite so crisp and delicate of execution, and this is most noticeable in the figure sculpture. In the basement mouldings, as in the temple of Lakshmī-Nārāyaṇa at Pedgāon, occurs the horse-moulding above that of the elephants, and, thus, it contains the full complement of mouldings provided in the canons of architecture as followed in North Gujarāt. There is a double row of images which could only be introduced upon the larger buildings of this class. The whole of the whitewashed roof is of much later work. (Plates CXIII—CXV.)

The half lotus band, just above the band of little figures at the top of the basement, is unusual, and although a regular Gujarāt ornament, it is seldom found in that province upon old buildings before the Hindu architects introduced it largely into the decoration of the mosques and tombs which they raised for their Muhammadan conquerors.[1] The pillars remind one much of some of those in the thirteenth century temple of Tejahpāla at Dilwārā on Mount Ābu. They have lost the more graceful outline of those of the eleventh century.

[1] It occurs on the old temple at the Hirā Gate at Dabhoi, of A.D. 1253.

The floor of the shrine is considerably sunk below that of the hall, and the *liṅga* is thus not seen from the hall doorway.

There is at Aundha the ruins of an old brick temple, in which the bricks have been carefully moulded to the contour of the ornamental bands which run round the building. The bricks are exceptionally well made and their edges are sharp and crisp. A small amount of stone masonry has been used in the entrance doorway and the beams, as well as in a low moulded plinth upon which the temple stands.

# APPENDIX.

## PURI.

(*See mention of Purī on page 1.*)

THE identification or location of the ancient Śilāhāra capital, Purī, presents some difficulty owing to the few and meagre references to it in old inscriptions. In the earliest mention of the city, in a copper-plate grant of A.D. 584, and the stone inscription on the ancient temple of Meguṭi at Aihoḷe of A.D. 634,[1] we are told that Chaṇḍadaṇḍa, the general of Pulikeśi II, conquered the Mauryas of the Koṅkaṇ and attacked the city of Purī—the Lakshmī or Goddess of the Fortunes of the Western Ocean, and presumably their capital —with hundreds of ships.[2] A later mention of Purī is found in an inscription in cave 78 at Kanheri, of the reign of the Rāshṭrakūṭa king Amoghavarsha, dated in A.D. 843-44, which records that his feudatory, the *Mahāsāmanta*, Pullaśakti, of the northern branch of the Śilāhāras, was then governing the whole Koṅkaṇ, "headed by the city of Puri," which he held through the favour of his suzerain lord.[3] There is no reason to doubt that the Purī of the Maurya period was the same as that of the Śilāhāra. Purī is also mentioned in other inscriptions in connection with the Śilāhāras (A. D. 843-1187). In these it is stated that Purī was the chief city of a district of 1,400 villages.

Places that have been mentioned as possible sites of the old capital are Thāna, Kalyān, Supāra, Chaul, Mangalapurī or Māgāthān in Sālsette island, Rājāpuri in the Janjira State down the coast, Purī near Bassein and Ghārāpurī on Elephanta island. As Thāna, Supāra and Chaul occur as separately named places in the same inscriptions with Purī they may be at once dismissed. Kalyān is too far inland for a sea-girt capital.[4] Rājāpurī and Purī have no remains to indicate an ancient capital. Moreover, there would have been no occasion for Chaṇḍadaṇḍa to have had recourse to his navy to attack Purī had it occupied either of these places, as they would have been more conveniently reached by land. And Ghārāpurī, upon Elephanta, in the Bombay harbour, will not do, for an exhaustive examination of the island has shewn that there could never have been any town or city of any size or importance upon it. The central portion of the island is occupied with high hills which

[1] *Indian Antiquary*, V. 70, 72; 276; VIII, 237; IX, 44 and XII.

[2] See *Bombay Gazetteer*, Vol. XIV, part 3, p. 401, and Vol. I, part 2, p. 16, note 2.

[3] *Indian Antiquary*, Vol. XIII, p. 136.

[4] In the *Kumdrapāla Charittra*, the Śilāhāra capital is described as the sea-girt Shatāndpuri.

spread themselves out towards the three corners of the island, the greatest

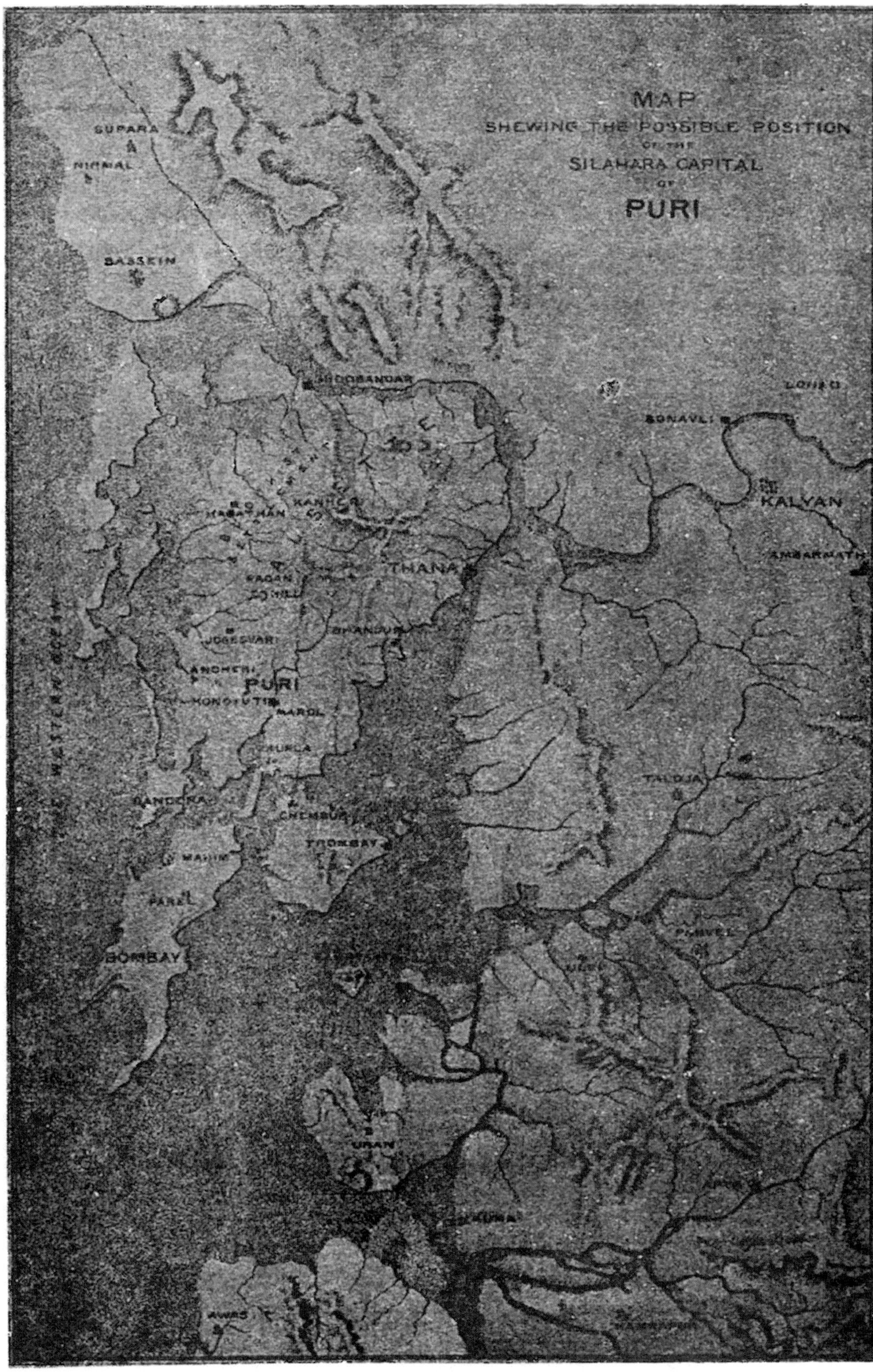


Fig. 17.

length of which, measured from one extreme corner to the other, being less than one mile and a quarter. In the middle of the north-west and south-west sides, and along the north-eastern, the hills recede somewhat from the shore, leaving three, more or less, level areas which are now occupied by rice fields and the hamlets of Shetbandar, Ghārāpurī and Moreh, respectively. But these areas, when lumped together, hardly exceed half a square mile—scarcely sufficient to accommodate a city and such forces as would require a hundred ships to attack them. From the remains upon the island, it would appear to have been always a religious settlement, first of the Buddhists, and afterwards of the Brahmanical communities. Another very serious objection is that during the greater part of the monsoon the island is cut off to a great extent by rough seas.[1]

There is, however, another site, and a much more likely one, for the city of Purī, and that is in the middle of Sālsette island (See the accompanying sketch map). The island is literally sea-girt, but at the same time the north and north-east sides are not so far separated from the mainland as to have made it difficult for the Śilāhāras to have transported their troops one way or the other. This site, about a mile north of Marol village, is bounded by the Sālsette hills on the north, by a long ridge, in which are the Kondivte caves, on the west, a stream on the east, and Marol village on the south. It is now filled with low rice fields between irregular areas of rocky waste ground, covered to a great extent with cocoanut palms and brush-wood jungle. Upon some of these latter spaces are vestiges of former Hindu temples of the fourteenth or fifteenth century. The site has, however, been almost wiped clean by the Portuguese, who found, in the ruins of the old temples, abundant material with which to erect their numerous churches and convents, which themselves, in turn, are now in ruins or have disappeared altogether. Near the centre of the site, on the west side of an old tank, around which are indications of old buildings, a trial excavation revealed the buried foundations of two old buildings of considerable size, one having been supported on pillars set in groups of four. A few hundred yards to the east is the Sarpala tank, on the east side of which are a few sculptured fragments and mutilated images of a Hindu temple; and, in the wall across the outflow, at the south end, are built several more fragments. On the south of these two tanks are some seven or eight sites, with the remains of foundations cropping up, and there is another, with a much-corroded boundary stone, upon the hill to the east of these. Other ruins are of the Portuguese period.

Mr. S. M. Edwards, I.C.S., in an article contributed to *East and West*, for April, 1902, sought to show that this same site which he calls "The Dead City of Shashti," was that of Partappur or Pratappur which Marathi records state was built near the centre of Shashti (Salsette) by Pratapdeva or Partapdeva, son of Bhimadeva, who fled from Devagiri to Salsette on the approach of 'Ala-ud-dīn Khilji.

[1] See the Progress Report of the Archæological Survey of Western India for the year ending 30th June 1921, p. 9, for a full account of the remains on the island, and a map of the same.

# GLOSSARY.

ĀKŚVARA.—An epithet of Śiva.

AGNI.—The god of fire, and guardian of the south-east point of the compass.

AMRITEŚVARA.—" The Lord of Nectar," a name of Śiva.

AÑJANĪ.—The mother of Mārutī.

ARDHACHANDRA.—" Half-moon," the ornamental semicircular step before a shrine doorway.

ASṬADIKPĀLAS.—The eight guardians of the eight points of the compass.

AŚVATHARA.—An architectural term, the horse moulding in the basement of some mediæval temples.

AVATĀRA.—An incarnation.

BĀLĀJI.—A name of Kṛishṇa, especially during his boyhood.

BALEŚVARA.—" The Lord of Might," a name of Śiva.

BHAIRAVA.—The terrific form of Śiva.

BHAVĀNĪ.—A name of Pārvatī.

BRĀHMĀ.—The first deity of the Hindu trinity.

BRĀHMĪ.—The *sakti* or female counterpart of Brāhmà.

CHAITYA.—The term applied to the arched-roofed caves of the Buddhists.

CHANDRĀPRABHA.—One of the *tīrthankaras* or saints of the Jains.

CHĀNGADEVA.—The name of an ancient *sādhu* or Hindu saint.

CHĀVADI.—The open court-house of a village.

CHHATRA or CHHATRI.—An umbrella, a pavilion.

DĀGOBA.—A representation or model of a burial mound, such as were built over the ashes or relics of the Buddha.

DEVA.—A god. Also used as a suffix to the names of kings and distinguished persons.

DEVĪ.—A goddess. Also used as a suffix to the names of queens and princesses.

DHARMAŚĀLĀ.—A charitable rest house.

DIGAMBARA.—One of the sects of the Jains whose images are nude; also a name of Śiva in his nude form.

DIKPĀLA.—A guardian of one of the points of the compass. See " *Asṭadikpālas.*"

DURGĀ.—A name of Pārvatī.

DVĀRAPĀLA.—A door-keeper; also a name of Vishṇu.

GAJA-LAKSHMĪ.—The goddess Lakshmī as represented with two elephants, one on either side of her, pouring water upon her head from vessels held in their trunks.

GAṆA.—Śiva's attendants, generally represented as a troop of imps.

**Gaṇapati** or **Gaṇeśa**.—The god of wisdom and son of Śiva and Pārvatī, and the leader of Śiva's *gaṇa*.

**Gangā**.—The river Ganges, personified as a goddess.

**Garuḍa**.—The *vāhana* or vehicle of Vishṇu, and the son of Kaśyapa by his wife Vinatā.

**Ghāt**.—A mountain pass, or a flight of steps by the side of a river or tank.

**Gopī**.—A cowherd's wife, a milkmaid.

**Gopura**.—A lofty many-storied gateway to a temple enclosure, very common in Southern India.

**Garāsmukha**.—The same as *kīrtimukha*, a grotesque face used as a decoration upon mouldings, pillars and other parts.

**Garāspatti**.—The particular string-course or moulding in the basement of temples, decorated with the *garāsmukha*.

**Hanumān**.—The chief of the monkey warriors, worshipped as a demi-god.

**Hāṭakeśvara**.—An epithet of Śiva (*Hāṭaka*, gold).

**Hemāḍpanti**.—A style of temple architecture supposed to have been introduced by Hemāḍpant or Hemāḍri, a minister to the Yādava king of Devagiri in the thirteenth century.

**Indra**.—The lord of gods, and the guardian of the east.

**Īśa**.—An epithet of Śiva, and guardian of the north-east.

**Jagadambā**.—A name of Durgā as "Mother of the Universe."

**Jāgeśvara**.—An epithet of Śiva.

**Jakaṇāchārya**.—The mythical builder of temples in the south.

**Jalandhara**.—An *āsura* or demon, son of the Ocean and Gaṇgā, and slain by Śiva.

**Jain**.—A follower of the Jinas; a religious sect whose doctrines are somewhat similar to those of the Buddhists.

**Jaṅghā**.—The thigh; an architectural term applied to the broad band of sculpture upon the walls of a temple above the basement.

**Jatrā**.—A fair, held periodically.

**Jina**.—A term applied to each of the twenty-four, past, present and future holy teachers or *tīrthankaras* of the Jains.

**Jyotirliṅga**.—The term applied to any one of the twelve most celebrated *lias* in India.

**Kalaśa**.—A pot; also the pot-like finial of the spire of a temple.

**Kaṇi**.—An architectural term for the knife-edge moulding in a temple basement.

**Kīrtimukha**.—The same as *garāsmukha*; a grotesque face, much used in decorative details. For its origin see page 12.

**Krishṇa**.—One of the incarnations of Vishṇu.

**Kuṇḍa**.—A reservoir or tank.

**Kuvera**.—The god of wealth and guardian of the south.

LAKSHMĪ.—The wife of Vishṇu and goddess of wealth.

LAKSHMĪ-NĀRĀYAṆA.—Lakshmī with Nārāyaṇa or Vishṇu. She is generally represented as seated on his lap.

LIṄGA.—The genital organ of Śiva, worshipped in the form of the phallus.

MAHĀDEVA.—A favourite epithet of Śiva as the "Great God."

MAHĀKĀLĪ.—Durgā in her terrible form.

MAHĀSĀMANTA.—A tributary prince or governor.

MAHISHĀSURA-MARDANĪ.—Durgā, who killed the demon Maheśa.

MAKARA.—A conventionalised beast used in decorative detail. For a description of it see page 12.

MAṆḌAPA.—The large hall of a temple.

MAṬHA.—A monastery.

MIHRĀB.—The niche in the centre of the back wall of a mosque, towards which worshippers turn when at prayer.

NĀGA.—A serpent; the chief of the serpent race, generally represented with a human body to the waist and a serpent tail, said to inhabit Pātāla, the nether world.

NANDI.—The sacred bull of Śiva, and his constant attendant and vehicle.

NARASIṀHA.—The man-lion *avatāra* of Vishṇu.

NARATHARA.—One of the mouldings in the basement of a temple, decorated with images of men.

NĀRĀYAṆA.—Vishṇu.

NATEŚVARA or NATEŚA.—Śiva in his rôle as a dancer.

NIRṚITI.—The guardian of the south-west and personification of decay or destruction.

PANCHALIṄGA.—A collection of five *liṅgas*; or a *liṅga* with five heads on it.

PANCHĀYATANA.—Five deities, generally Śiva, Vishṇu, Gaṇapati, Sūrya and Devī.

PĀṆḌAVAS.—The five sons of king Pāṇḍu, namely, Dharma, Bhīma, Arjuna, Nakula and Sahadeva.

PĀRŚVANĀTHA.—One of the twenty-four present *tīrthankaras* of the Jains.

PĀRVATĪ.—The wife of Śiva, the mountain-born.

PIṆḌE.—The same as *liṅga*.

PRADAKSHIṆĀ.—Circumambulation from left to right, so that the right hand is always towards the object circumambulated.

PURĀṆAS.—Old traditional stories, eighteen in number.

RAKHMĀI.—The wife of Viṭhoba.

RĀMĀYAṆA.—The celebrated epic by Vālmiki in seven *kāndas* or books.

RĀMEŚVARA.—An epithet of Śiva.

REṆUKĀ.—The wife of Jamadagni and mother of Paraśurāma.

ṚISHABHADEVA.—The first of the present twenty-four *tīrthnkaras* of the Jains.

SAKA.—The Hindu era of Salivāhana.

ŚĀLUNKĀ.—The stone within which the *linga* is placed, and which represents the female counterpart of the *linga*.

SAMĀDHA.—A tomb.

ŚAMBHU.—Śiva.

SAMVAT.—The Hindu era of Vikrama.

SANGAMEŚVARA.—An epithet of Śiva.

SAPTAMĀTṚĪS.—The seven divine mothers, namely, Brahmī, Maheśvarī, Kaumārī, Vaishṇavī Māhendrī or Aindrī, Vārāhī and Chāmuṇḍī.

SARASVATĪ.—The goddess of learning and letters, and the wife of Brahmā; also a name of Durgā.

SATĪ.—A name of Durgā; a wife who immolates herself on her husband's funeral pyre.

ŚESHA.—A serpent-deity.

SIDDHEŚVARA.—An epithet of Śiva (*Siddha*, perfected).

ŚIKHARA.—A mountain peak, or the spire of a temple.

ŚIVA.—The third deity of the triad (Brāhmā, Vishṇu and Śiva).

SOMEŚVARA or SOMANĀTHA.—An epithet of Śiva (Lord of the Moon).

ŚRĪ.—Lakshmī; also used as a prefix to works and writings and to the names of great persons.

STŪPA.—A Buddhist monument erected to hold sacred relics.

SUNDAR-NĀRĀYAṆA.—Vishṇu.

SŪRYA.—The Sun-god.

TĀṆḌAVA.—An extraordinary dance of Śiva.

TIRTHANKARA.—A Jaina saint. There are supposed to be twenty-four of them in the past, twenty-four in the present, and twenty-four in the future dispensations.

TRIMŪRTI.—A triad representation of the gods Brahmā, Vishṇu and Śiva.

VĀHANA.—A vehicle. Each of the gods has his own particular *vāhana* upon which he rides.

VARĀHA.—Third or Boar incarnation of Vishṇu.

VARUṆA.—The god of the waters, and guardian of the west.

VĀYU.—The god of the winds, and the guardian of the north-west.

VIRAGAL or VIRAKAL.—A memorial stone set up in commemoration of the death of a warrior.

VIRŪPĀKSHA.—Śiva (having an unusual number of eyes).

VISHṆU.—The second god of the Hindu Triad.

VIṬHOBĀ.—A form of Vishṇu, the celebrated god of Paṇdarpur.

VIṬṬHALA.—The same as the last.

YAMA.—The god of death, and guardian of the south.

YAMUNĀ.—The Jamnā river personified as a goddess.

YOGI.—A religious ascetic.

MGIPC—M—X-3-9—25-2-27—600.

PLATE I

SRI GANESA.

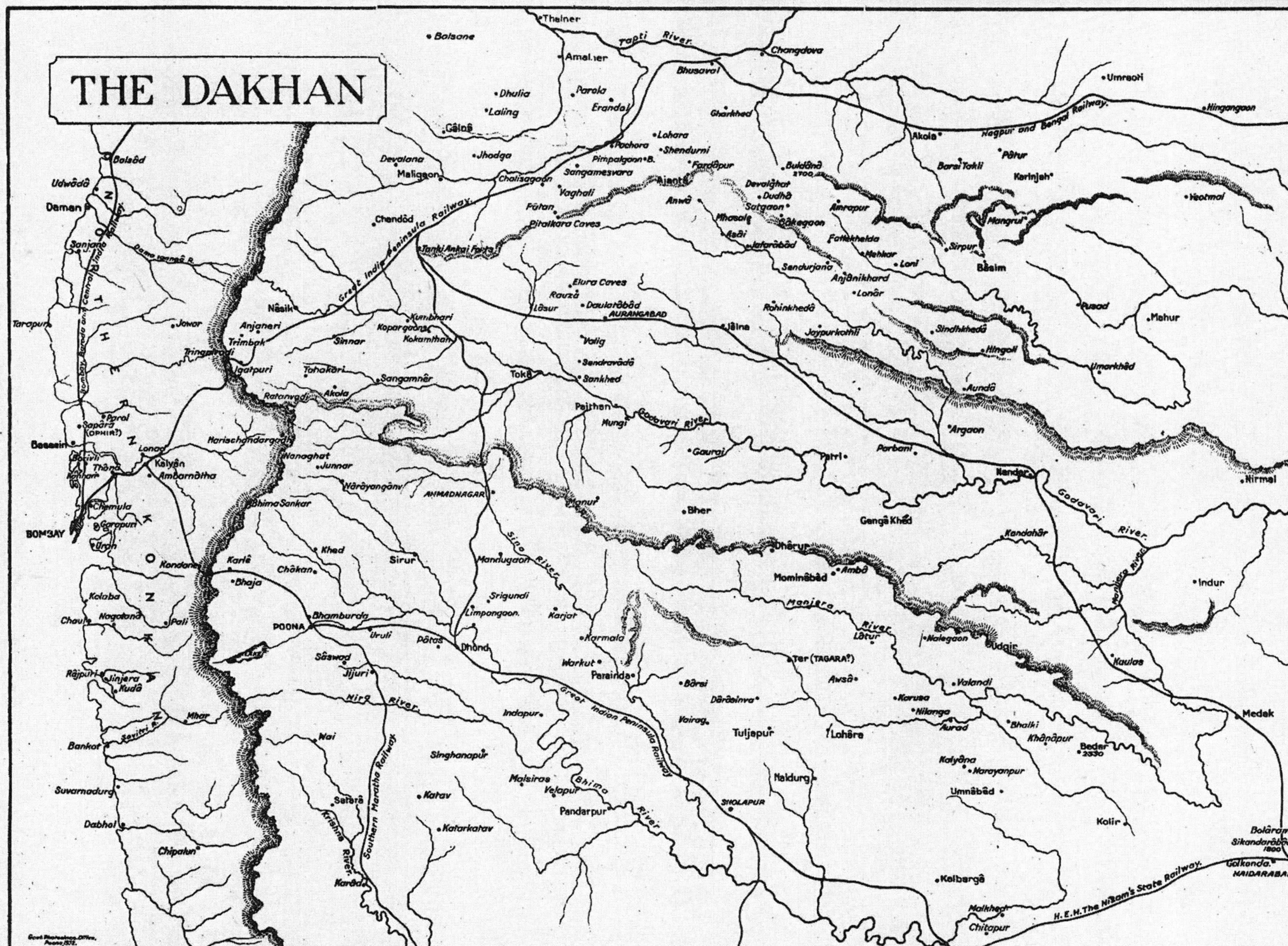
THE DAKHAN
Thalner
Tapti River.
Bolsone
Amalner
Changdova
Bhusaval
Umraoti
Dhulia
Parola
Laling
Erandal
Gharkhed
Nagpur and Bengal Railway.
Hingangaon
Gâlnâ
Lohara
Pachora
Shendurni
Akola
Pâtur
Balsâd
Devalana
Jhodga
Pimpalgaon B.
Buldânâ
Barsi Takli
Karinjah
Maligaon
Chalisagaon
Sangamesvara
Fardâpur
Udwâdâ
Vaghali
Ajantâ
Devalghat
Dudhâ
Yeotmal
Daman
Anwâ
Satgaon
Amrapur
Chendôd
Fûtan
Mhasala
Dâkegaon
Mangrul
Pitalkara Caves
Asâi
Fattekhelda
Sanjana
Tanki Ankai Forts
Jafarâbâd
Mehkar
Sirpur
Great Indian Peninsula Railway.
Sandurjana
Loni
Basim
Anjânikhard
Elura Caves
Lonâr
Rauzâ
Daulatâbâd
Pusad
Mahur
Tarapur
Jowar
Nâsik
Lâsur
AURANGABAD
Rohinkhedâ
Anjaneri
Jâlna
Jayparkothli
Sindhkhedâ
Kopargaon
Kumbhari
Sinnar
Kokamthan
Trimbak
Valig
Hingoli
Tringalvadi
Igatpuri
Toka
Sendravâdâ
Umarkhed
Tohakari
Sankhed
Sangamnêr
Aundâ
Ratanvadi
Akola
Paithan
Parol
Mungi
Godavari River.
Sopara (OPHIR?)
Argaon
Bassein
Harischandargadh
Gaurai
Patri
Parbani
Borivli
Lonad
Nanaghat
Kalyân
Thâna
Junnar
Nander
Ambarnâtha
Kanheri
Nârâyangânv
AHMADNAGAR
Nirmal
Chemula
Bhima Sankar
Manur
Bher
Gangâ Khed
Gorapuri
BOMBAY
Uran
Khed
Sirur
Kandahâr
Godavari River.
Dhârur
Karlê
Châkan
Mandugaon
Mominâbâd
Ambâ
Kondane
Bhaja
Indur
Kolaba
Srigundi
Sina River
Limpongaon.
Karjat
Manjera River.
Chaul
Nagotanâ
Pali
Bhamburda
Manjera River
POONA
Lâtur
Uruli
Pâtas
Dhond
Karmala
Nalegaon
Udgir
Sâswad
Workut
Ter (TAGARA?)
Kaulas
Râjpuri
Jinjera
Kudâ
Jijuri
Parainda
Awsâ
Bârsi
Valandi
Dârâsinva
Karusa
Nira River.
Great Indian Peninsula Railway
Indapur
Nilanga
Medak
Mhar
Savitri R.
Wai
Vairag
Tuljapur
Lohâre
Aurad
Bhalki
Khânâpur
Bankot
Singhanapur
Beder 2330
Naldurg
Kalyâna
Narayanpur
Suvarnadurg
Malsiras
Velapur
Bhima River
Umnâbâd
Satârâ
Katav
SHOLAPUR
Pandarpur
Dabhol
Katarkatav
Kolir
Bolâram
Sikandarâbâd 1800
Chipalun
Krishna River.
Southern Maratha Railway.
Golkonda.
HAIDARABAD
Karâd
Kalbargâ
H.E.H. The Nizam's State Railway.
Malkhed
Chitapur
Govt. Photozinco. Office, Poona 1932.

PLATE III

NORTH FACADE OF THE TEMPLE OF AMBARNATHA.

PLATE IV

THE EASTERN END OF THE TEMPLE OF AMBARNATHA.

PLATE V

THE NORTH-WEST CORNER OF THE TEMPLE OF AMBARNATHA.

PLATE VI

IMAGES OF DURGA, BRAHMA AND MAHAKALI ON THE TEMPLE OF AMBARNATH.

PLATE VII

THE WALLS OF THE SHRINE OF THE TEMPLE OF AMBARNATHA

PLATE VIII

DOME IN THE HALL OF THE TEMPLE OF AMBARNATHA

PLAN OF THE TEMPLE OF AMBARNATHA.

QUARTER PLAN OF THE HALL CEILING OF AMBARNATHA.

CEILING PANELS IN THE HALL OF AMBARNATHA.

TWO PILLARS IN THE HALL OF AMBARNATHA.

IMAGE OF THE TRIMURTI ON THE TEMPLE OF AMBARNATHA.

PLATE XII

THE MOTHA TANKYA TEMPLE AND CARVED STONES FROM DEVI-KA-PARA

DOORWAY FROM THE MOTHA TANKYA TEMPLE AT PAROL.

PILLARS FROM THE LAHAN TANKYA TEMPLE AT PAROL.

STONE SCULPTURES FROM GAS AND NIRMAL.

PLATE XV

MEMORIAL STONES AT BORIVLI.

PLATE XVI

TEMPLE NO. 1 AT BALSANE. SOUTH FACE.

PLATE XVII

THE SHRINE WALLS OF TEMPLE NO. 1 AT BALSANE.

TEMPLE NO. 4 AT BALSANE.

PLATE XIX

INTERIOR OF TEMPLE NO. 2 AT BALSANE.

INTERIOR OF TEMPLE NO. 3 AT BALSANE

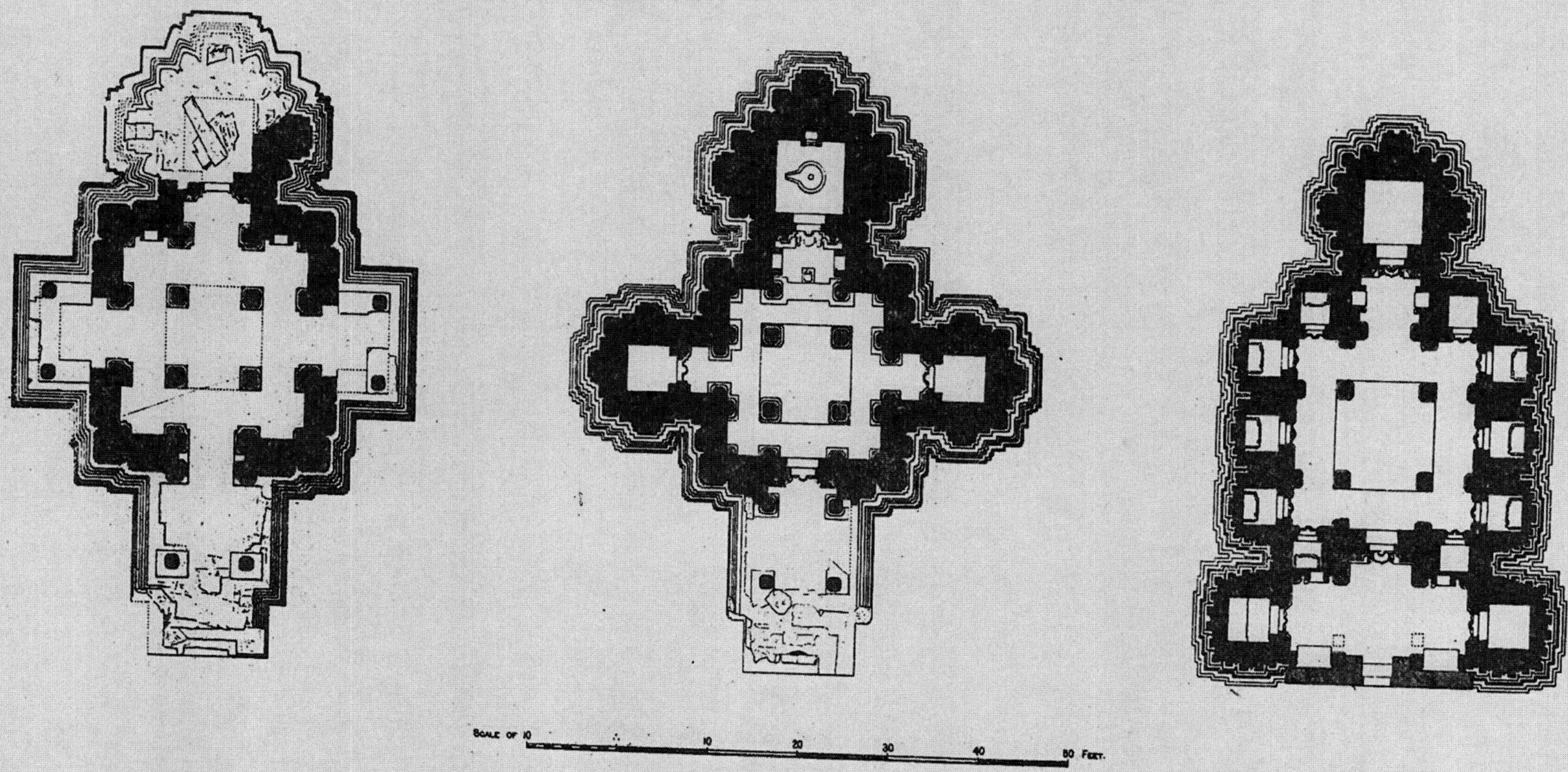


GROUND PLAN OF THE TEMPLES NOS. 4, 1 AND ↄ AT BALSANE.

PLATE XXII

ELEVATION OF TEMPLE NO. I AT BALSANE.

THREE PILLARS FROM TEMPLE NO. 1 AT BALSANE.

MOULDINGS OF MARGINAL CEILING OF HALL. FROM TEMPLE NO. 1 AT BALSANE.

PLATE XXIV

ELEVATION

SECTION

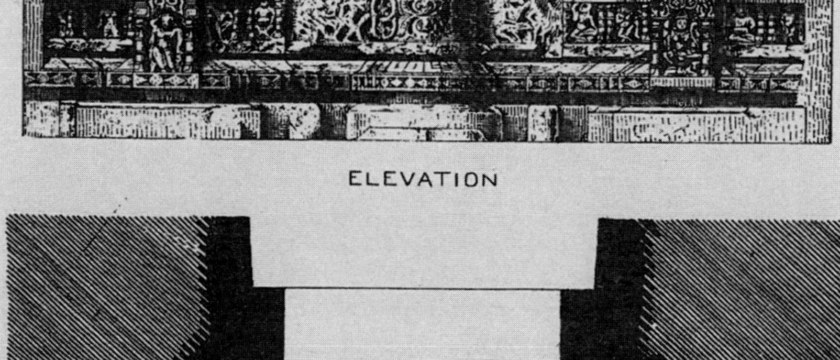

PLAN

SCALE OF 12" ... 1 2 3 4 5 6 7 8 9 10 FEET.

ELEVATION, PLAN AND SECTION OF DOORWAY OF TEMPLE NO. 1 AT BALSANE.

THE SOUTH SIDE OF THE TEMPLE OF MAHESVARA AT PATNA.

THE INTERIOR OF THE TEMPLE OF MAHESVARA AT PATNA.

THE TEMPLE AT SANGAMESVARA.

PLATE XXVII

THE TEMPLE OF MAHESVARA AT PATNA FROM THE NORTH-EAST

THE TEMPLE OF AI BHAVANI AT PATNA FROM THE BACK

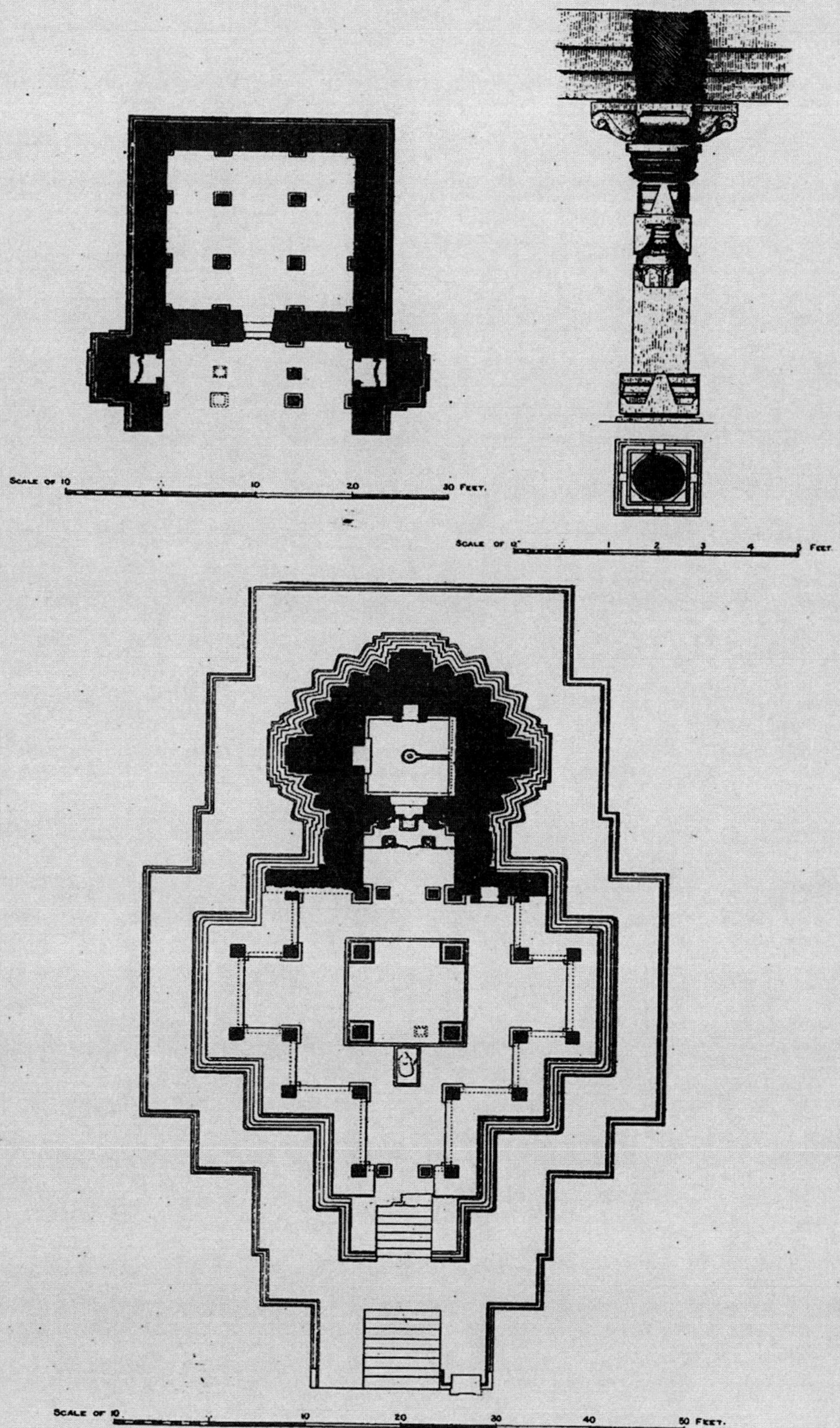


PLAN OF MATHA AND PILLAR FROM BALSANE, AND PLAN OF MAHESVARA AT PATNA.

PLATE XXIX

ELEVATION, SECTION AND PLAN OF THE SHRINE DOORWAY IN THE TEMPLE OF MAHESVARA AT PATNA.

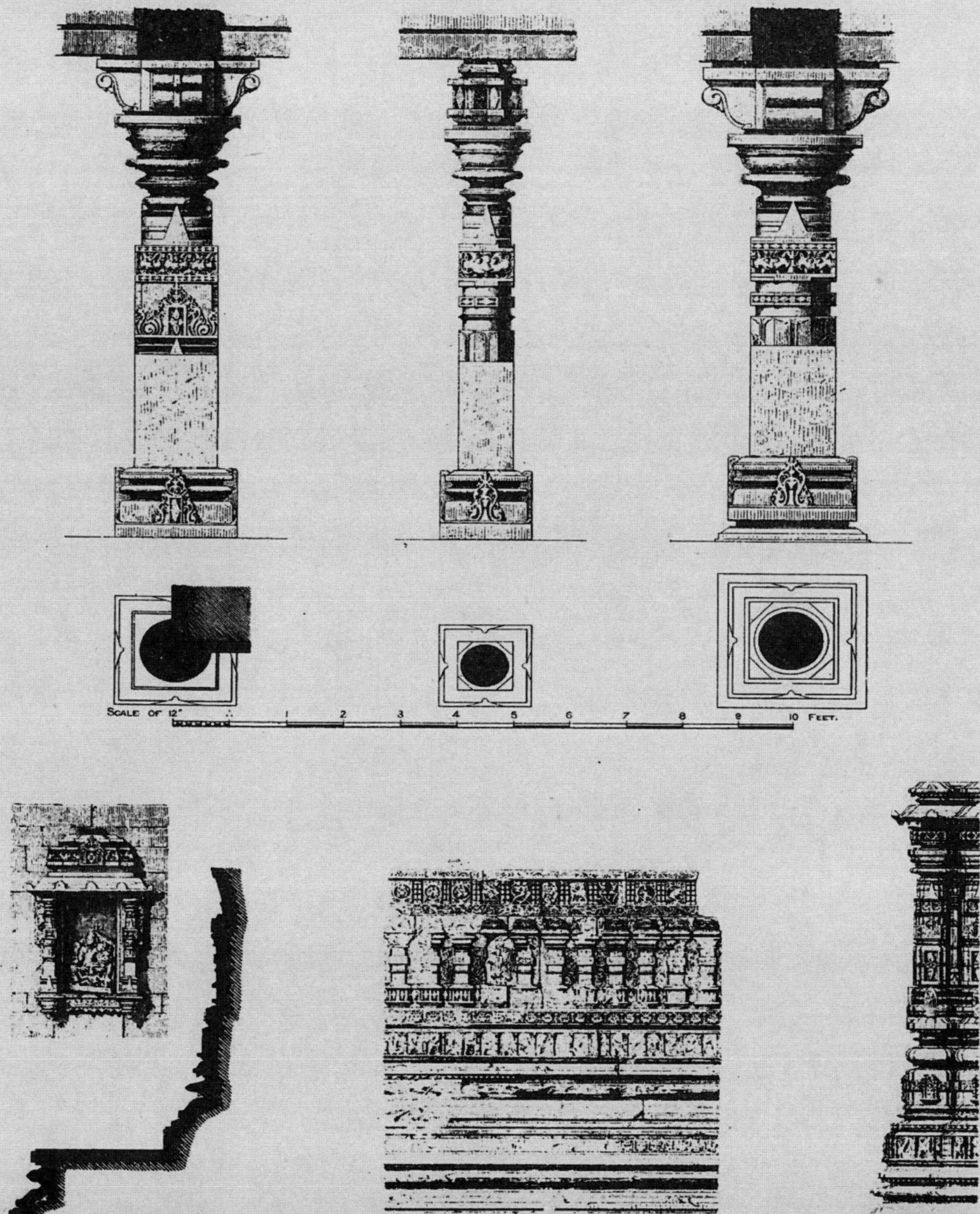


THREE PILLARS AND DETAIL OF WALL MOULDINGS FROM THE TEMPLE OF MAHESVARA AT PATNA.

BALCONIED NICHE AND STRING COURSES FROM MAHESVARA AT PATNA.

JAINA THRONE AND TWO AVATARAS OF VISHNU FROM PATNA.

SCALE OF 12" ∴ 1 2 3 4 5 6 7 8 9 10 FEET.

DOORWAY OF A SMALL TEMPLE ON THE SOUTH OF MAHESVARA AT PATNA.

THE TEMPLE OF MUDHAIDEVI AT VAGHLI FROM THE N-E.

THE TEMPLE OF MUDHAIDEVI AT VAGHLI FROM THE S-W.

PLATE XXXIV

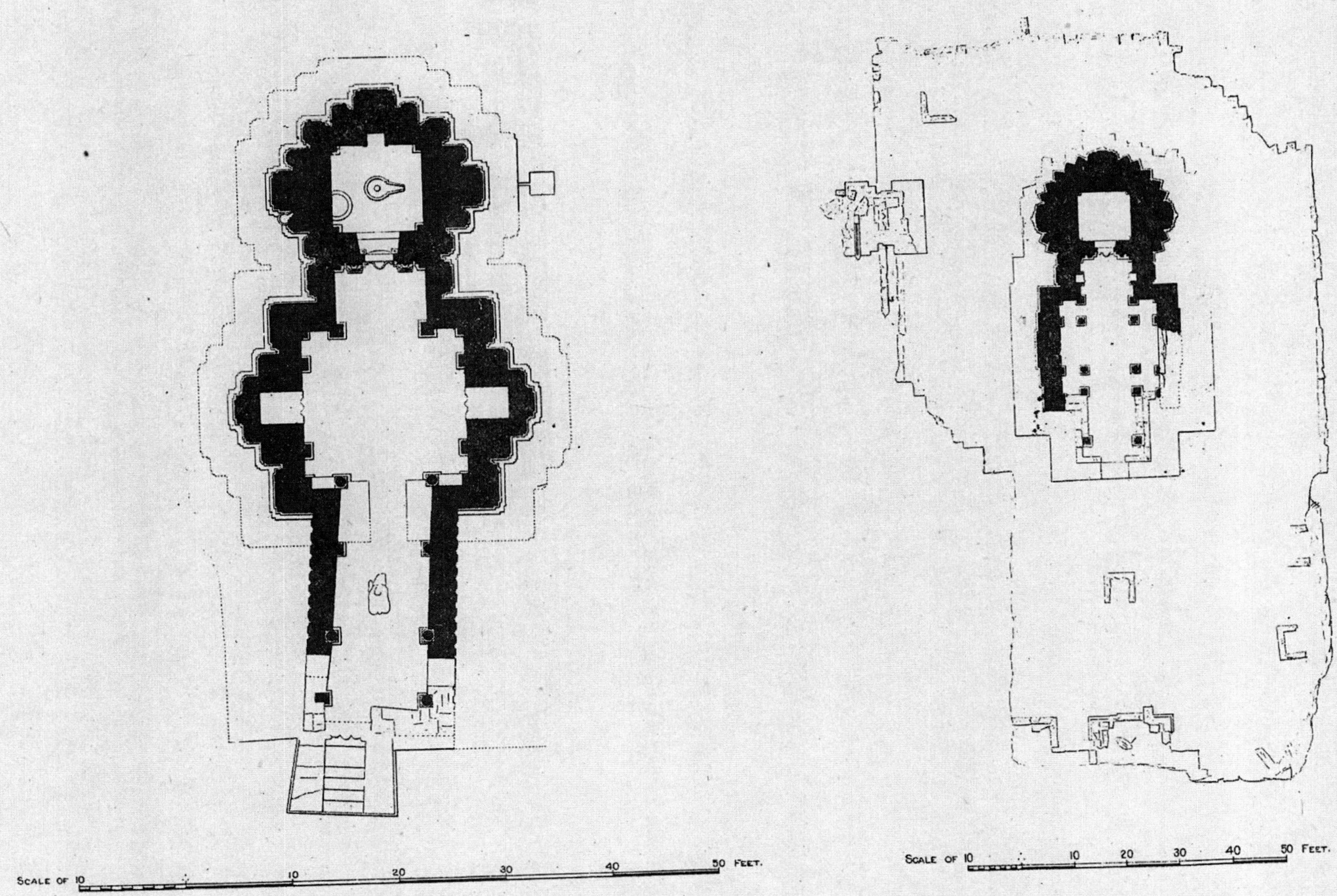


PLAN OF THE TEMPLE AT SANGAMESVARA, AND OF MUDHAIDEVI AT VAGHLI.

PLATE XXXV

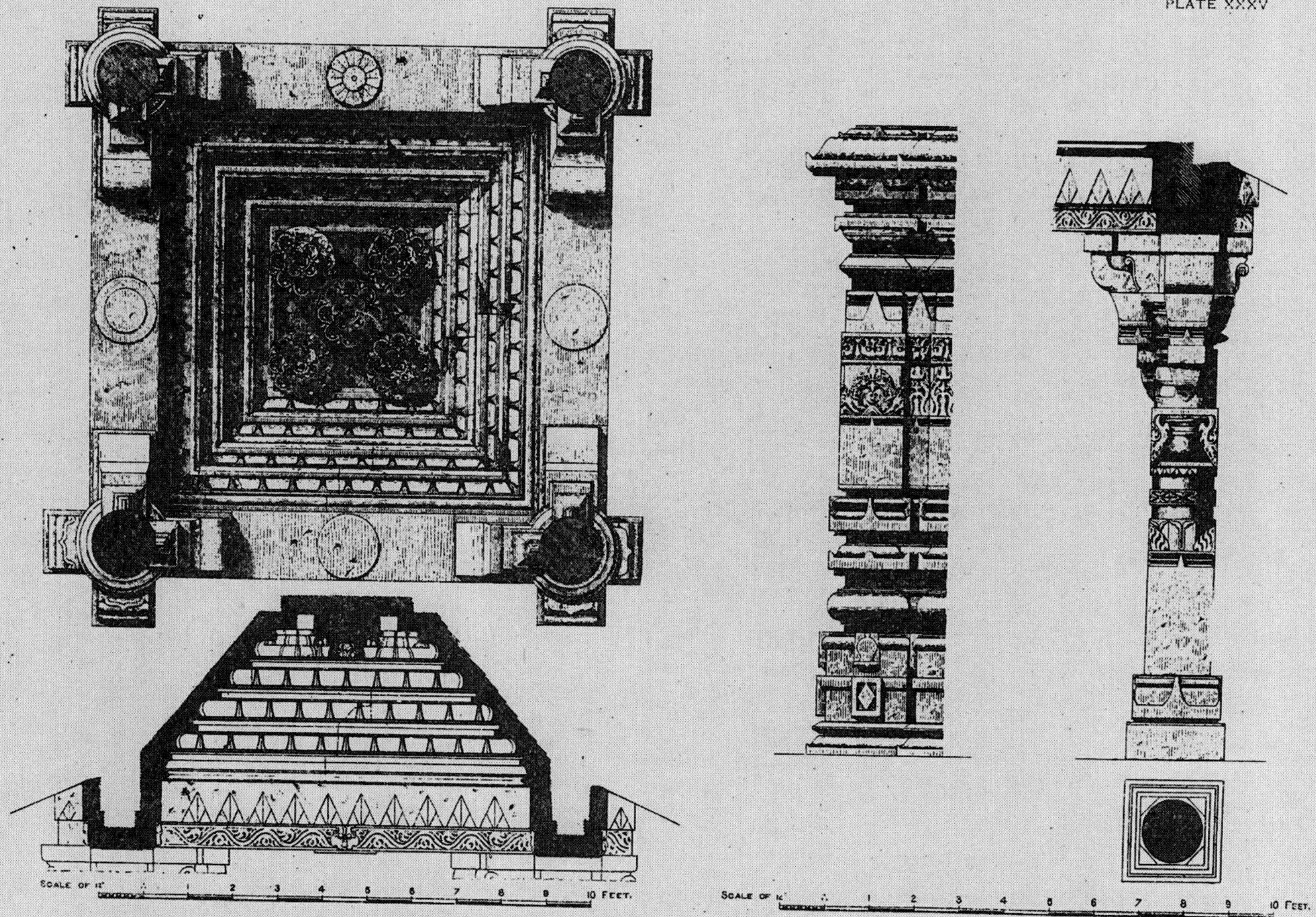

PLAN AND SECTION OF CEILING, AND PILLAR AND WALL MOULDINGS FROM THE TEMPLE OF MUDHAIDEVI AT VAGHLI.

PLATE XXXVI

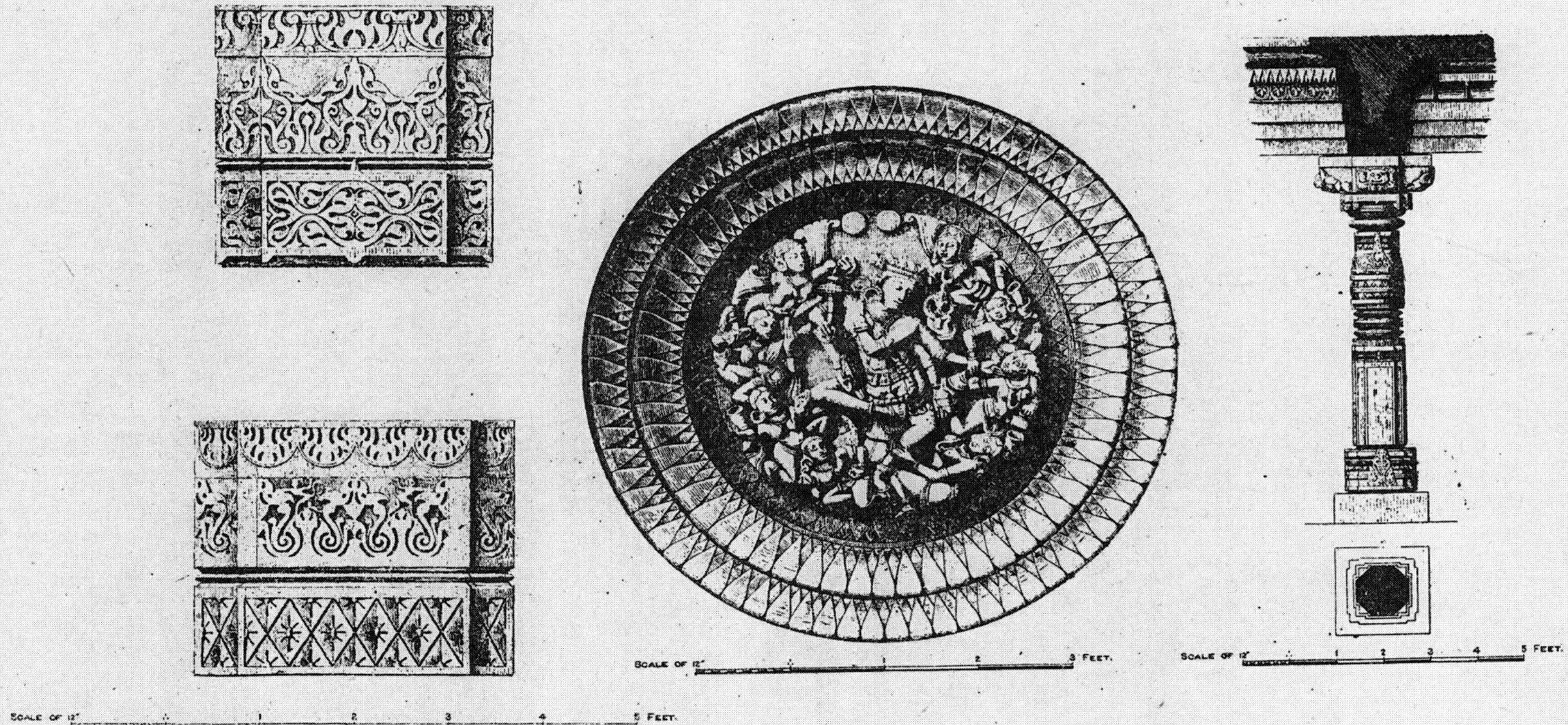


PANEL AND PILLAR FROM THE TEMPLE OF KRISHNA AT VAGHLI, AND DETAIL OF WALL BANDS FROM THE TEMPLE OF SANGAMESVARA.

PLATE XXXVII

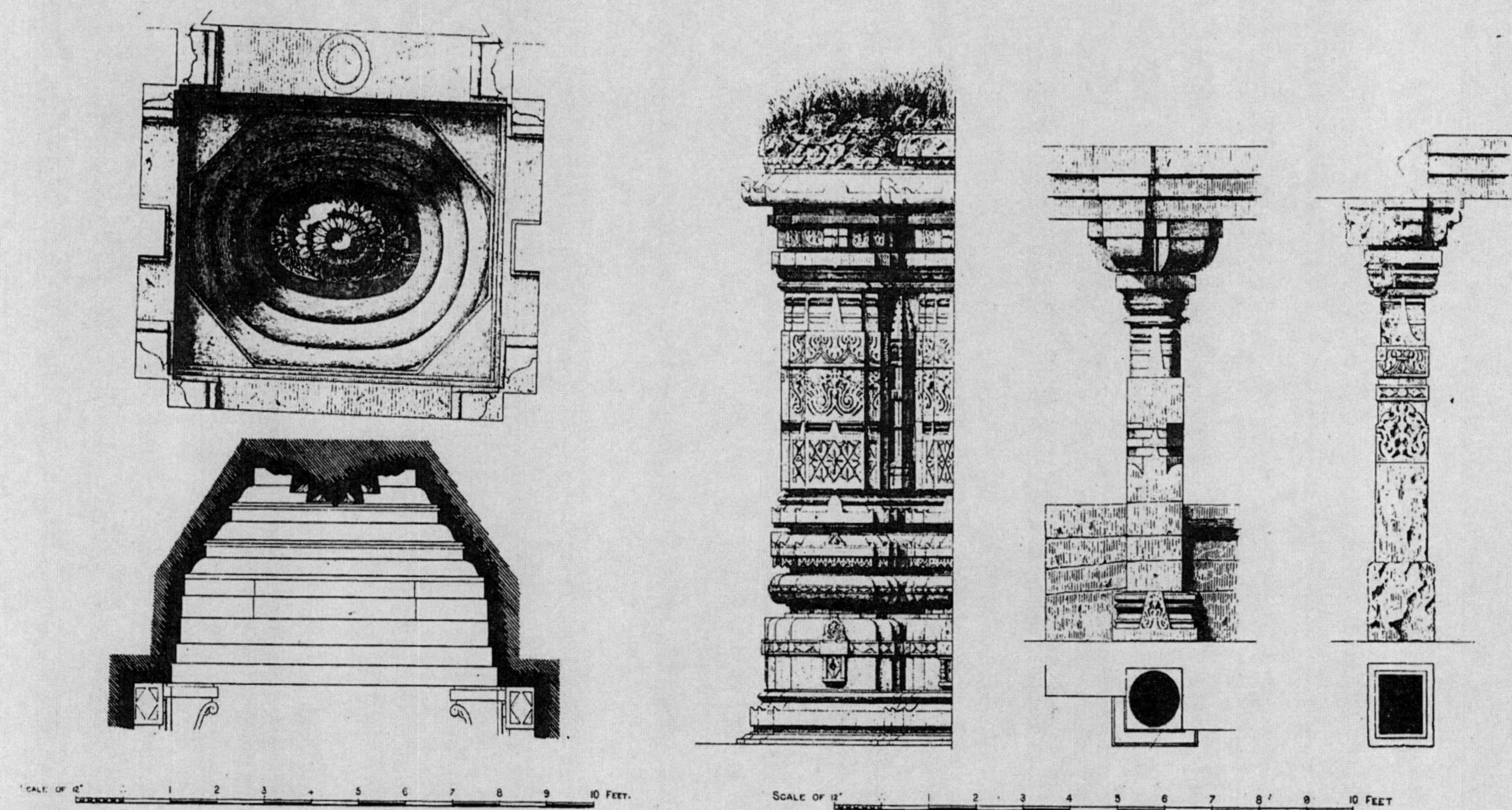


OVAL CEILING. WALL MOULDINGS AND PILLARS FROM SANGAMESVARA.

THE TEMPLE AT CHANGDEVA

THE FRONT OF THE ANTECHAMBER OF THE TEMPLE AT CHANGDEVA

THE TEMPLE IN THE BED OF THE RIVER AT CHANGDEVA.

PLAN OF THE TEMPLE OF CHANGDEVA, AND ELEVATION OF CORNER OF THE WEST WALL.

PLATE XLI

ELEVATION OF A MIHRAB AND DETAILS FROM THE PANDAVAS' WADA AT ERANDOL.

THE TEMPLE OF GONDESVARA AT SINNAR, FROM THE SOUTH.

TEMPLE OF GONDESVARA AT SINNAR FROM THE SOUTH-WEST.

THE TEMPLE OF AESVARA AT SINNAR.

PLATE XLIV

PORCH AND WALLS OF GONDESVARA AT SINNAR AND ACCOMPANYING SMALL TEMPLE

PLATE XLV

PILLAR FROM THE TEMPLE OF AESVARA, AND NANDI PAVILION FROM THE TEMPLE OF GONDESVARA AT SINNAR

PLATE XLVI

SCULPTURED ARCHITRAVE IN THE TEMPLE OF AESVARA AT SINNAR.

PLATE XLVII

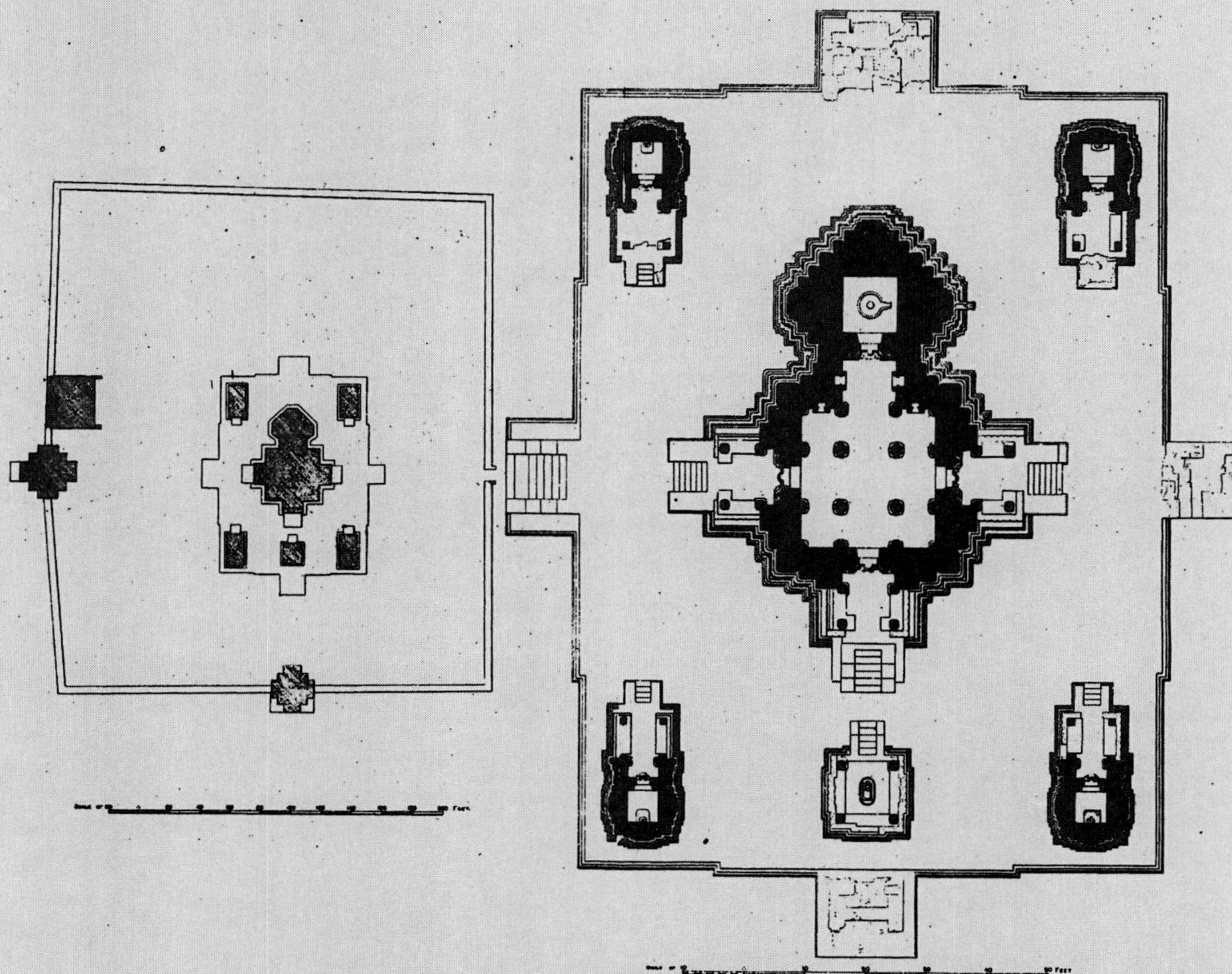

PLAN OF THE TEMPLE OF GONDESVARA AT SINNAR.

PLATE XLVIII

ELEVATION OF THE TEMPLE OF GONDESVARA AT SINNAR.

PLATE XLIX

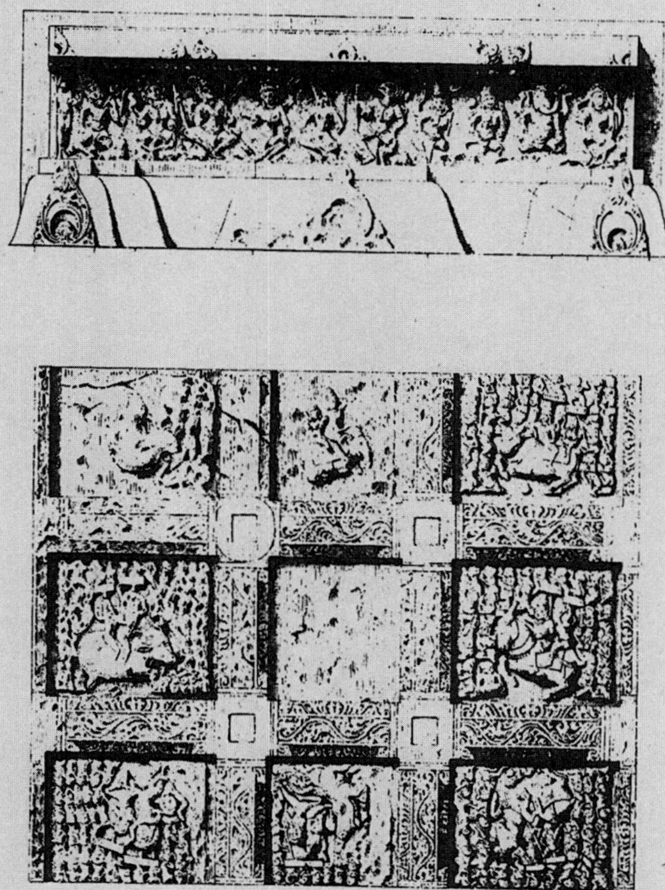

SCALE OF 12" ∴ 1 2 3 4 5 FEET. SCALE OF 10 ∴ 10 20 30 40 50 FEET.

ASHTADIKPALA CEILING FROM AESVARA, AND CROSS SECTION OF GONDESVARA AT SINNAR.

ELEVATION OF THE EAST DOORWAY OF THE HALL OF GONDESVARA AT SINNAR.

PLATE LI

PILLAR IN THE HALL OF GONDESVARA AT SINNAR.

PLATE LII

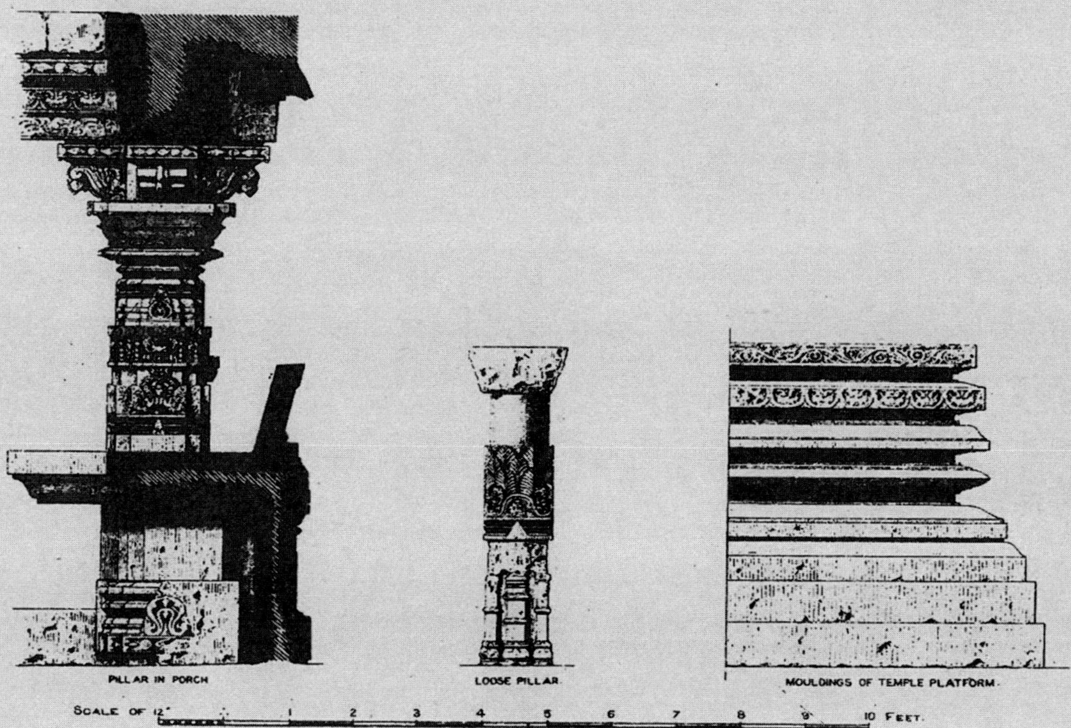


PILLARS FROM AESVARA, AND PILLAR AND MOULDINGS FROM GONDESVARA AT SINNAR.

PLATE LIII

TEMPLE AT JHODGA.

PLATE LIV

THE WALLS OF THE SHRINE OF THE TEMPLE AT JHODGA.

PLATE LV

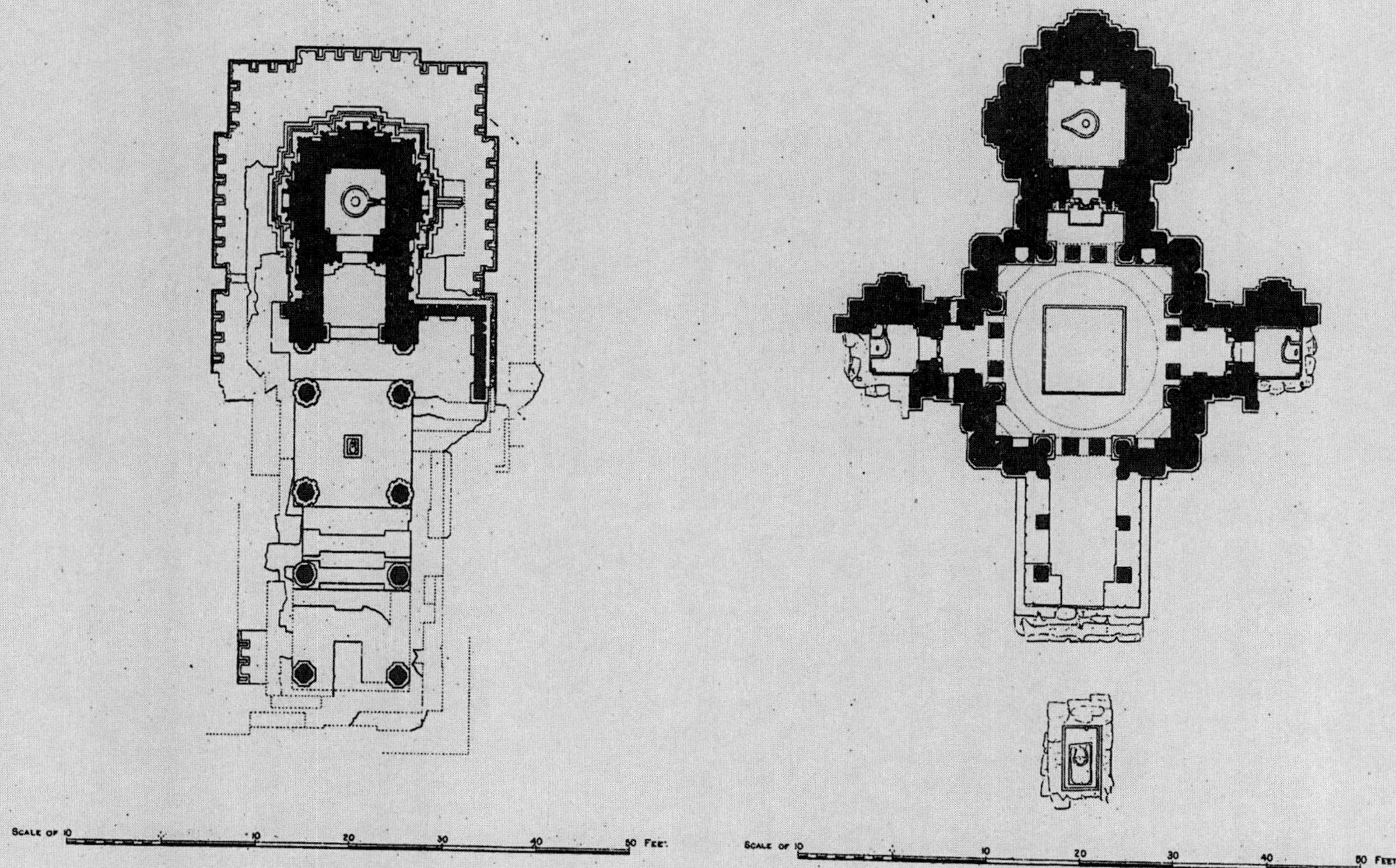


PLANS OF AESVARA AT SINNAR AND OF MAHADEVA AT JHODGA.

ORNAMENT ON THE FRONT OF THE SIKHARA AND PILLARS FROM THE TEMPLE AT JHODGA

PLATE LVII

TEMPLE NO. 8 AT ANJANERI.

TEMPLES NOS. 1 AND 2 AT ANJANERI.

TEMPLE NO. 7 AT ANJANERI.

PLATE LIX

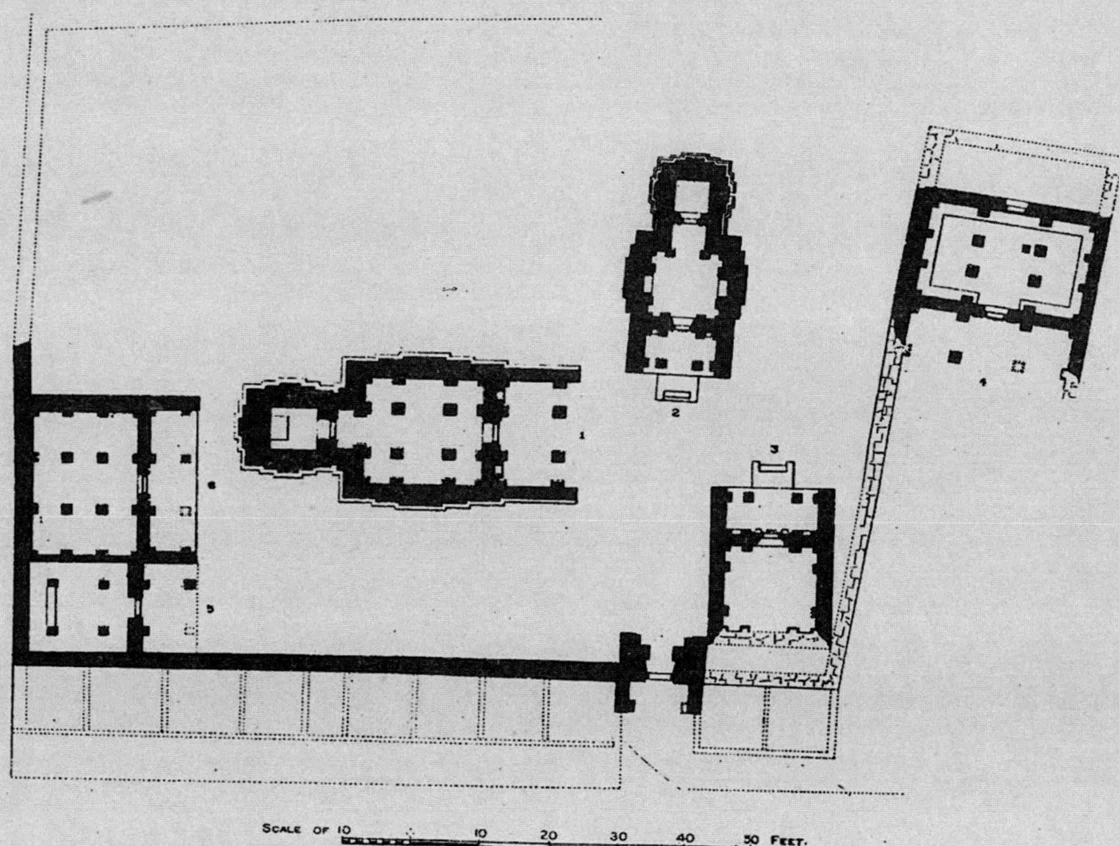


ELEVATION OF TEMPLE NO. 13 AT ANJAṆERI AND GENERAL PLAN OF GROUP OF TEMPLES.

DOORWAY, NICHE AND DOORSTEP OF TEMPLE NO. 2 AT ANJANERI.

PILLARS FROM THE GENERAL GROUP OF TEMPLES AT ANJANERI.

PLATE LXII

TEMPLE OF JOGESVARA AT DEVALANA

THE TRINGALVADI CAVE

PLATE LXIII

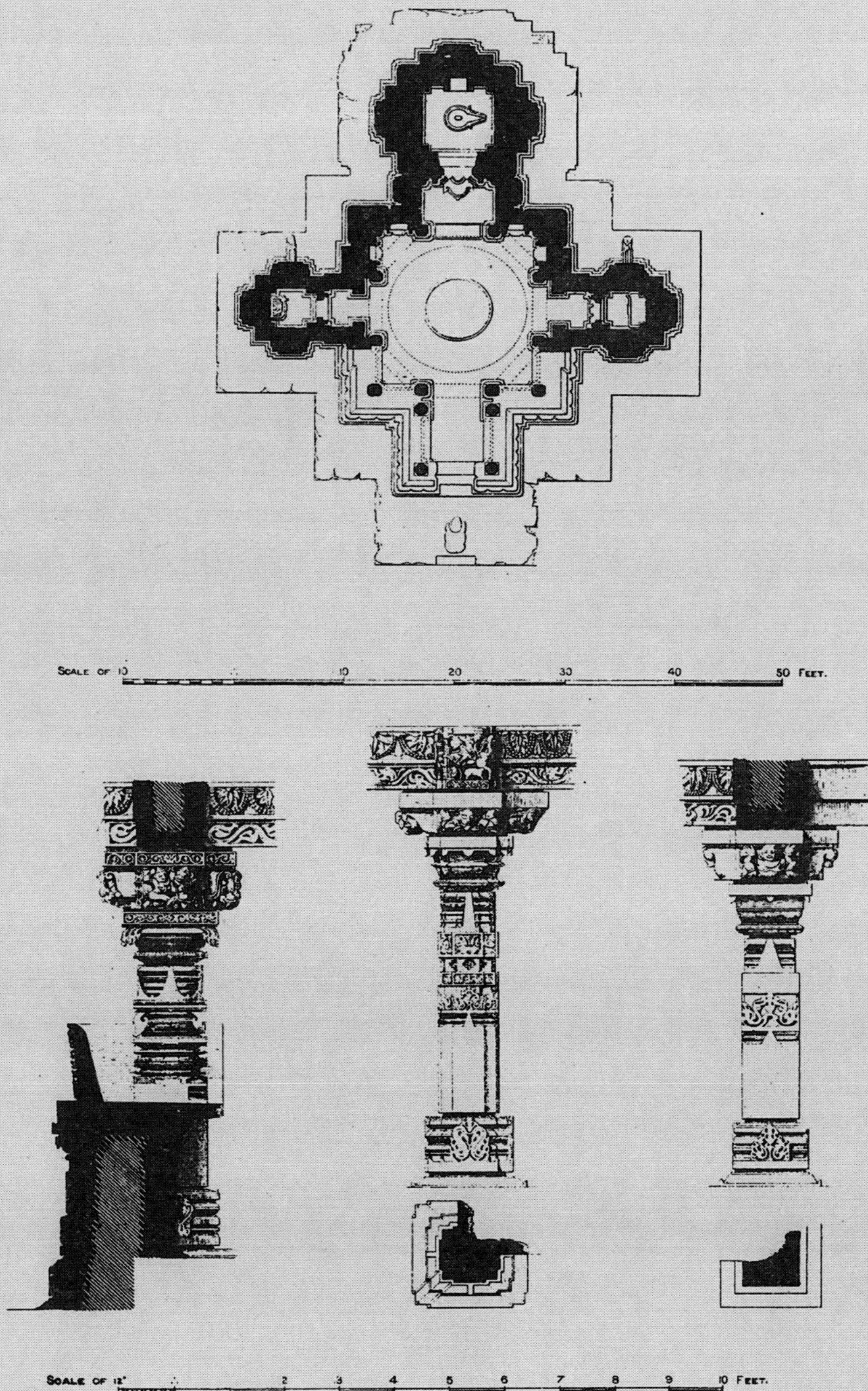


PLAN OF THE TEMPLE OF JOGESVARA AT DEVALANA AND PILLARS FROM THE SAME.

PLATE LXIV

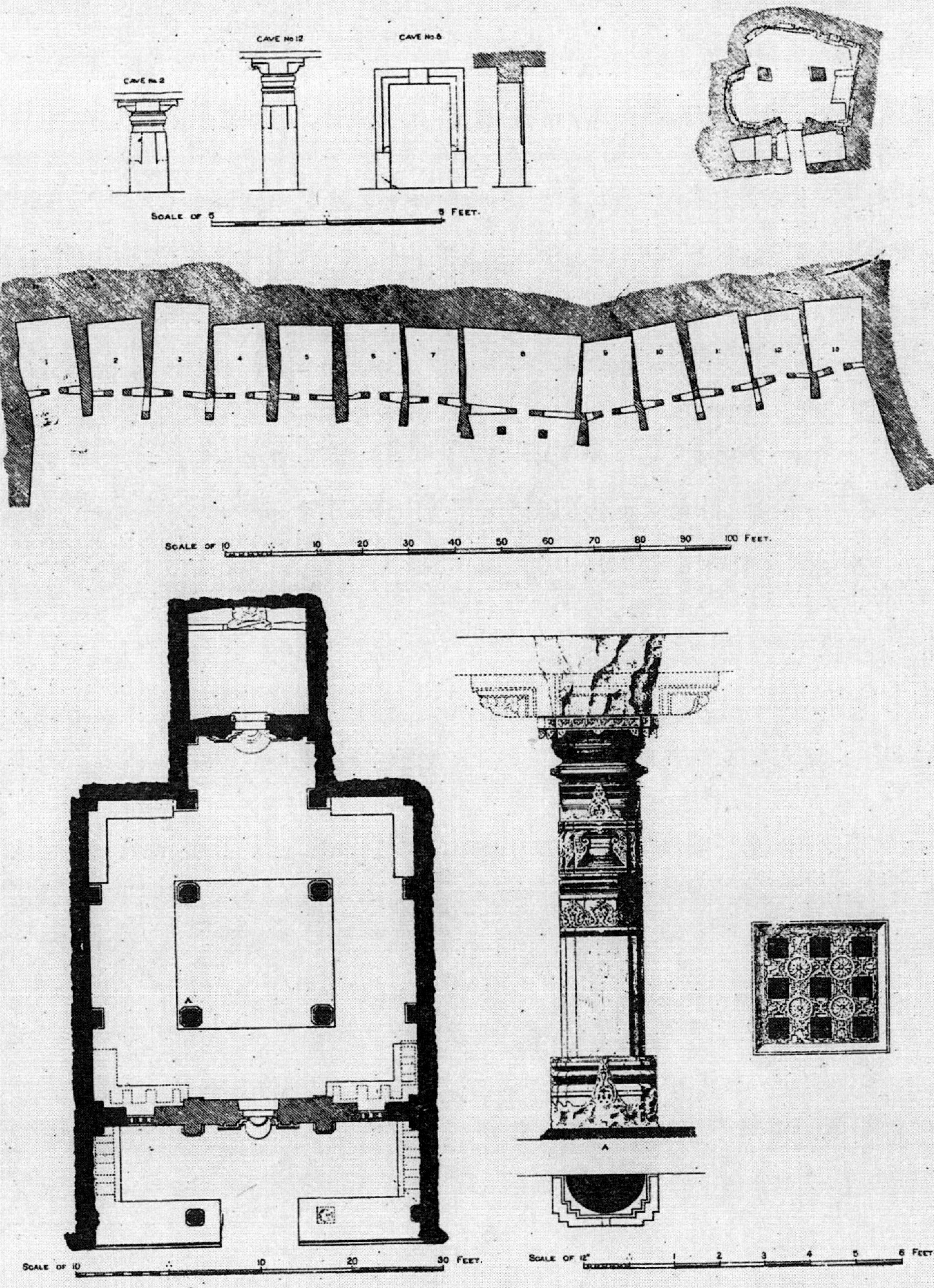


PLAN OF THE CAVES AT CHANDOR, AND PLAN OF TRINGALVADI CAVE, AND PILLARS.

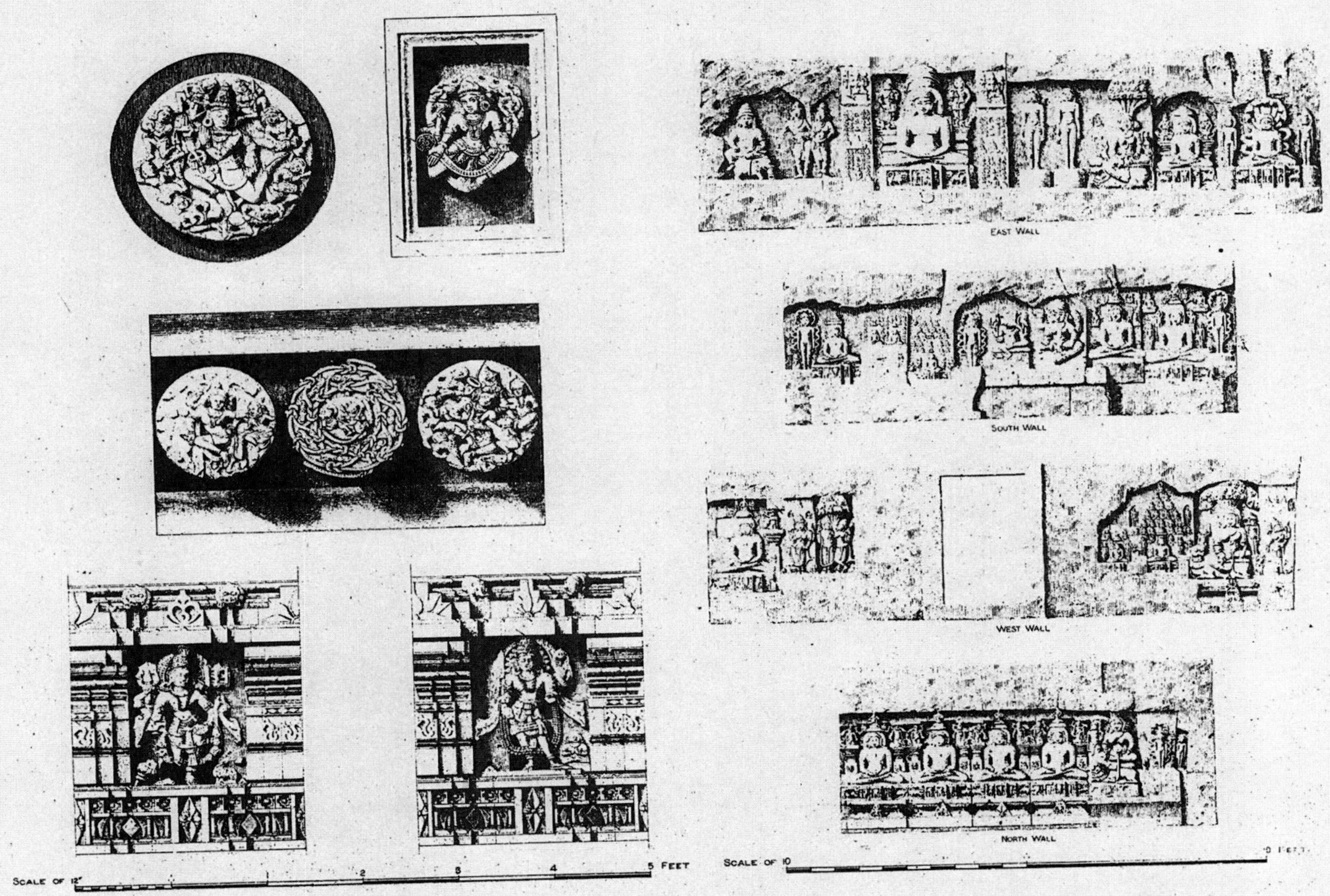


DETAILS OF SCULPTURES FROM TEMPLE OF JOGESVARA AT DEVALANA, AND FIGURES FROM THE JAINA CAVE AT CHANDOR.

WOODEN IMAGES OF ST. ANNE AND THE VIRGIN AT CHANDOR.

PLATE LXVII

THE TEMPLE OF JAGADAMBADEVI AT KOKAMTHAN

THE TEMPLE OF JAGADAMBADEVI AT KOKAMTHAN, FROM THE S-E.

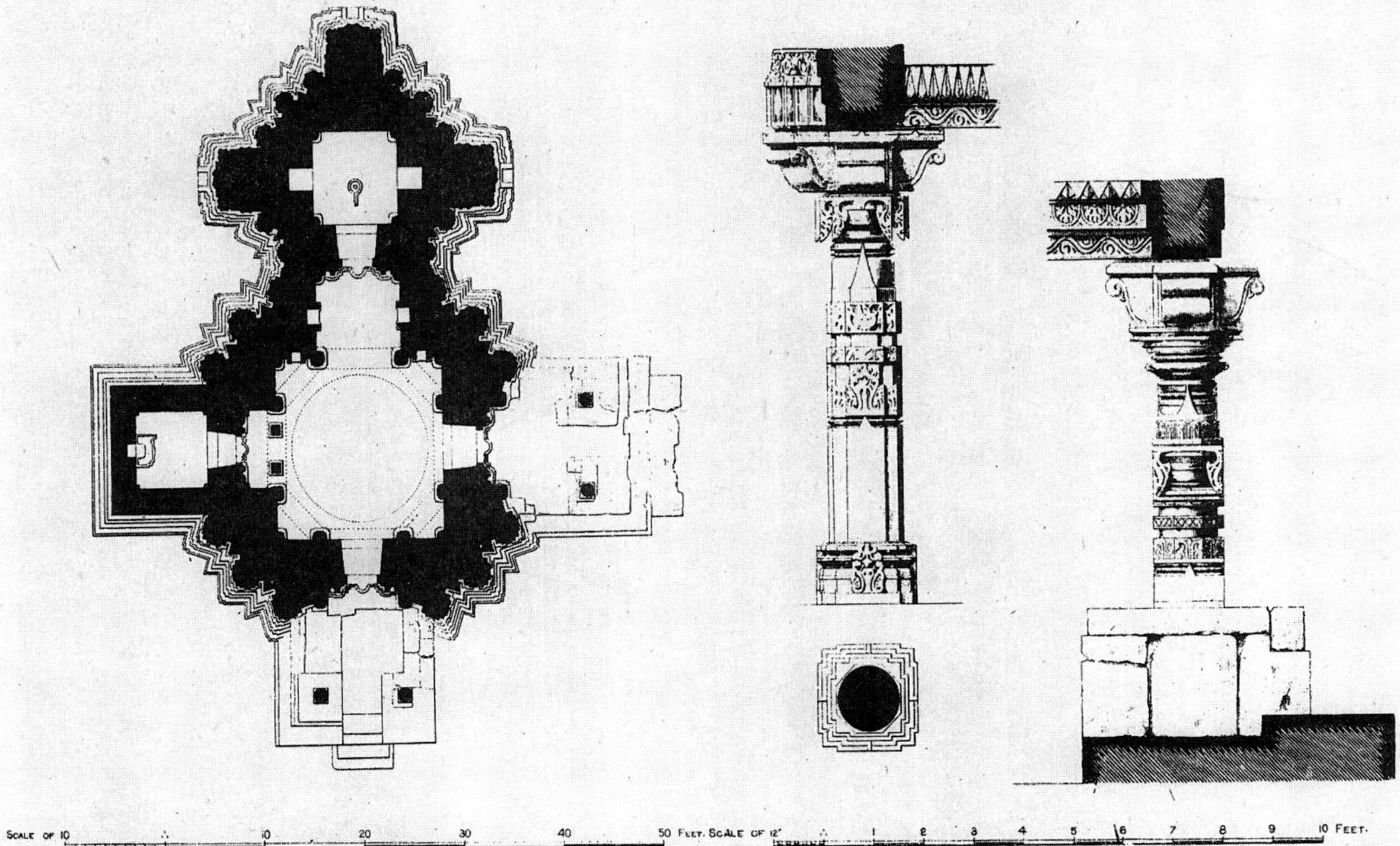


PLAN AND PILLARS OF THE TEMPLE OF JAGADAMBADEVI AT KOKAMTHAN.

TEMPLE OF SIDDHESVARA AT AKOLA

TEMPLE OF AMRITESVARA AT RATANVADI

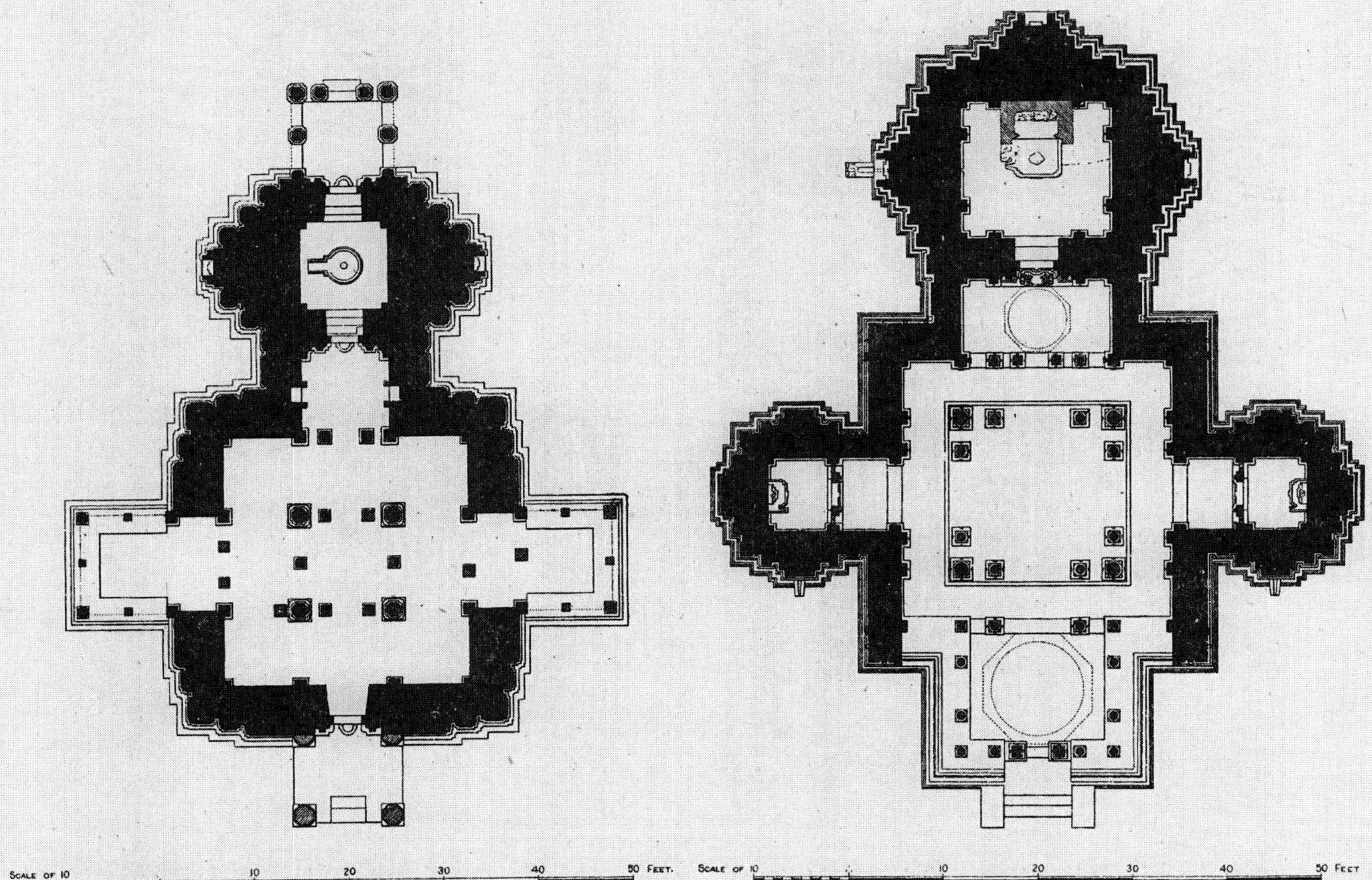


PLANS OF THE TEMPLE OF SIDDHESVARA AT AKOLA AND OF BHAVANI AT TAHAKARI.

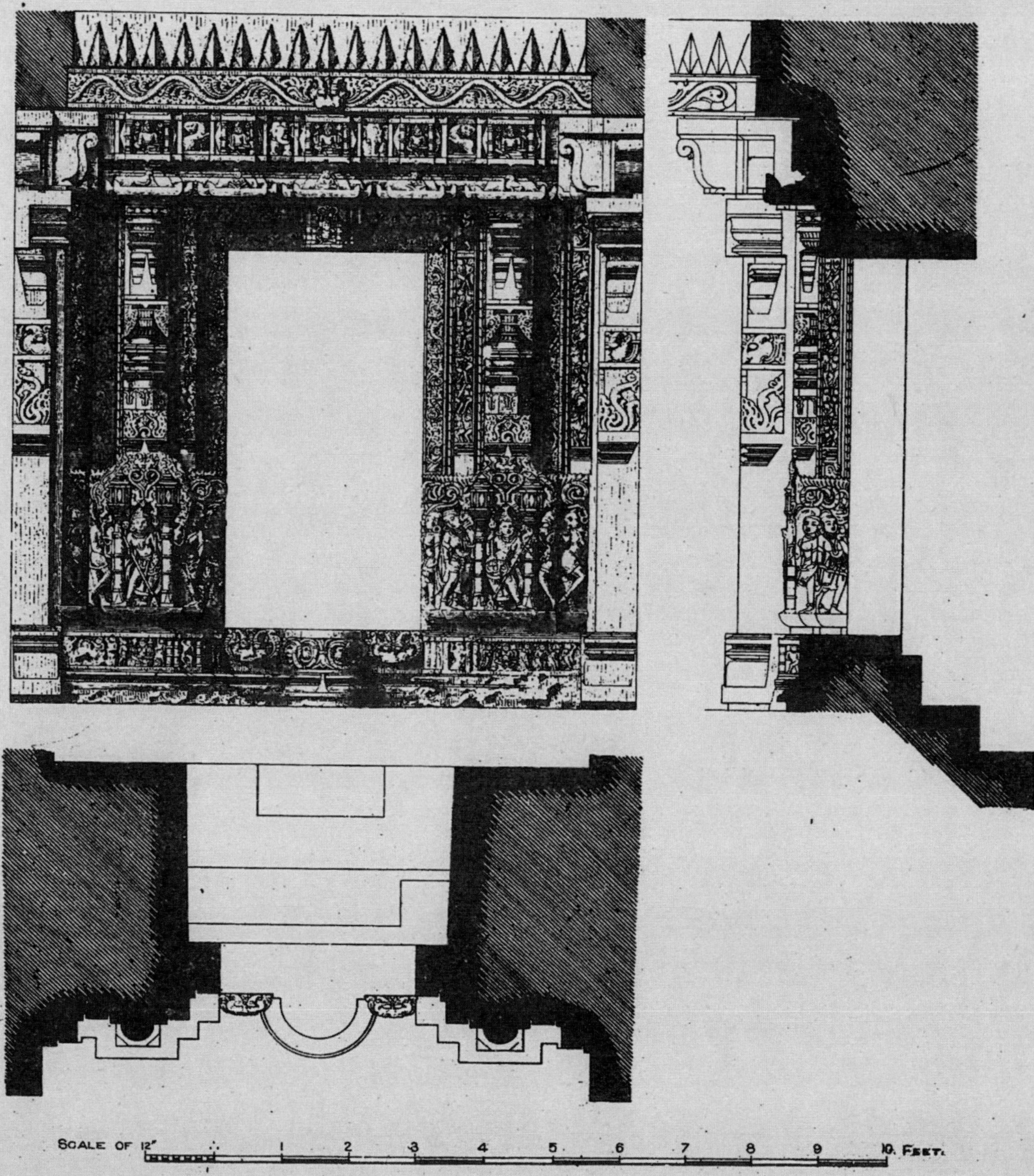


SHRINE DOORWAY OF THE TEMPLE OF SIDDHESVARA AT AKOLA.

PILLARS AND DETAILS FROM AKOLA AND TAHAKARI.

TEMPLE OF BHAVANI AT TAHAKARI

TEMPLE OF BALESVARA AT PEDGAON

PLAN AND SECTION OF DOMICAL CEILING IN THE TEMPLE OF BHAVANI AT TAHAKARI.

THE TEMPLE OF LAKSHMI-NARAYAN AT PEDGAON.

THE SHRINE WALLS OF THE TEMPLE OF LAKSHMI-NARAYANA AT PEDGAON.

CORNER OF THE WALL AND BASEMENT, AND PILLARS IN THE TEMPLE OF LAKSHMI-NARAYANA AT PEDGAON.

PLATE LXXIX

THE TEMPLE OF BALESVARA AT PEDGAON.

THE TEMPLE OF RAMESVARA AT PEDGAON.

PLATE LXXX

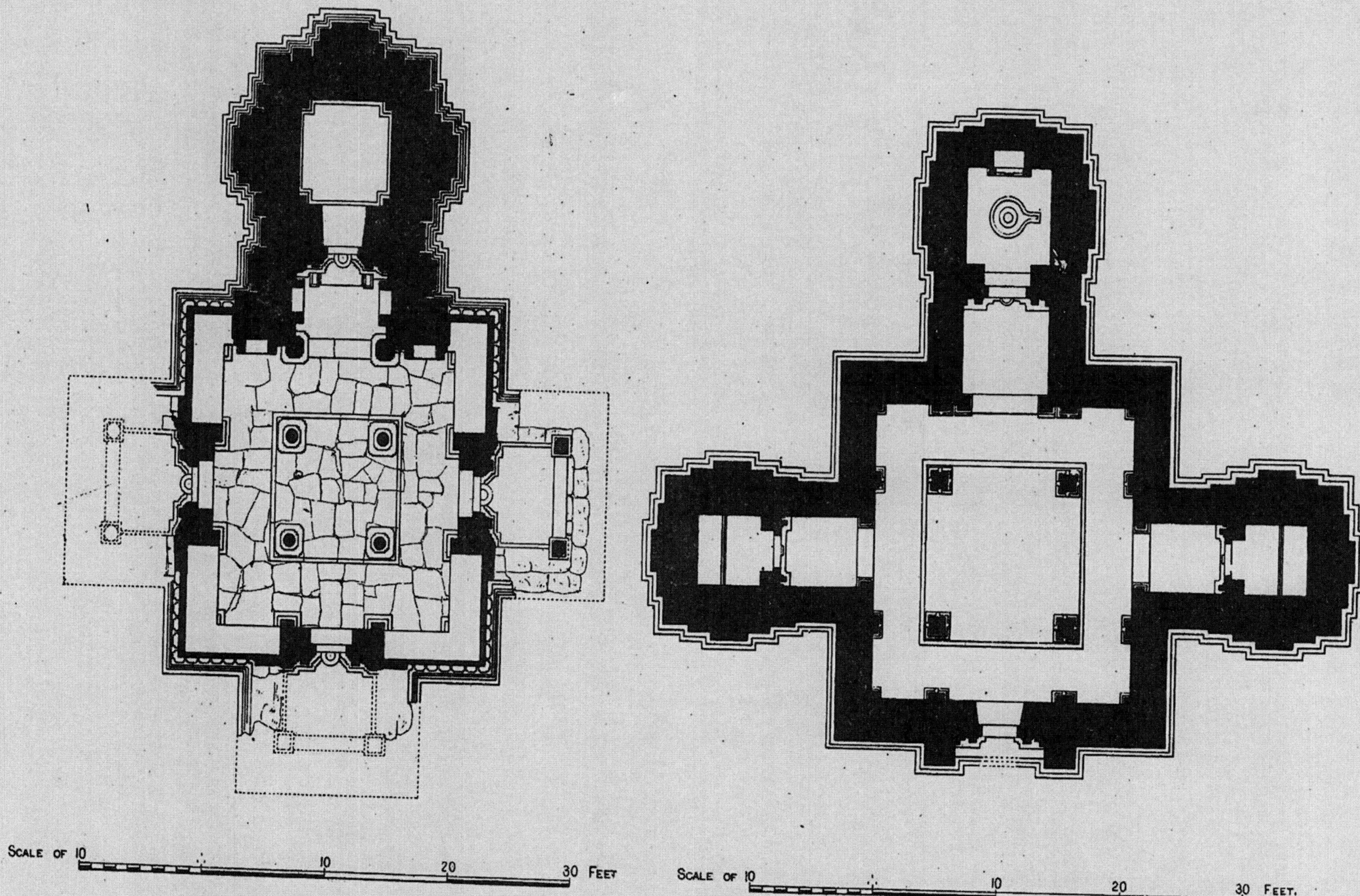


PLANS OF THE TEMPLES OF LAKSHMI-NARAYANA AND RAMESVARA AT PEDGAON.

PLATE LXXXI

ELEVATION OF THE TEMPLE OF LAKSHMI-NARAYANA AT PEDGAON.

ELEVATION, PLAN AND SECTION OF DOORWAY FROM THE TEMPLE OF LAKSHMI-NARAYANA AT PEDGAON.

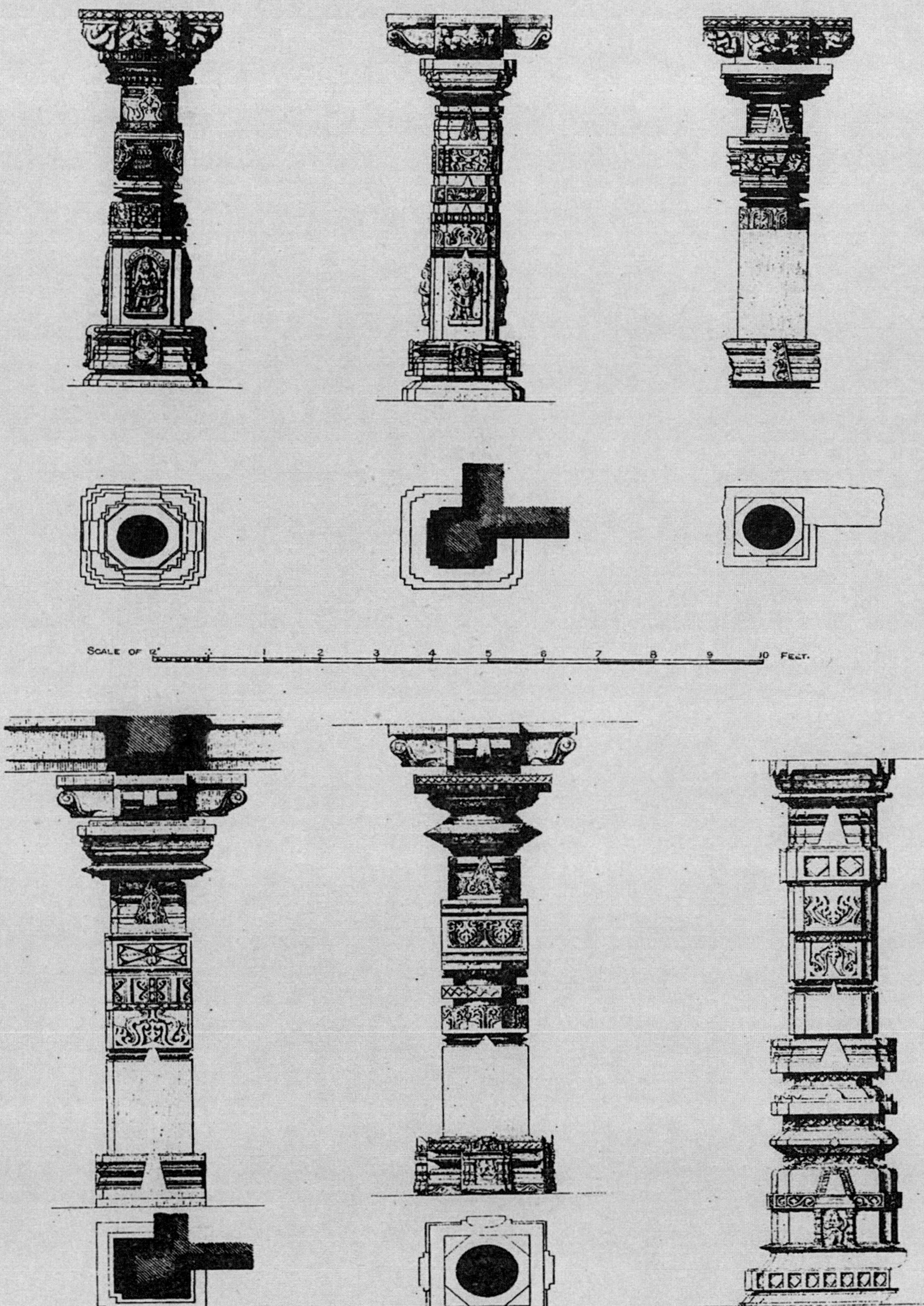


PILLARS FROM LAKSHMI-NARAYANA AND BALESVARA AT PEDGAON.

PLATE LXXXIV

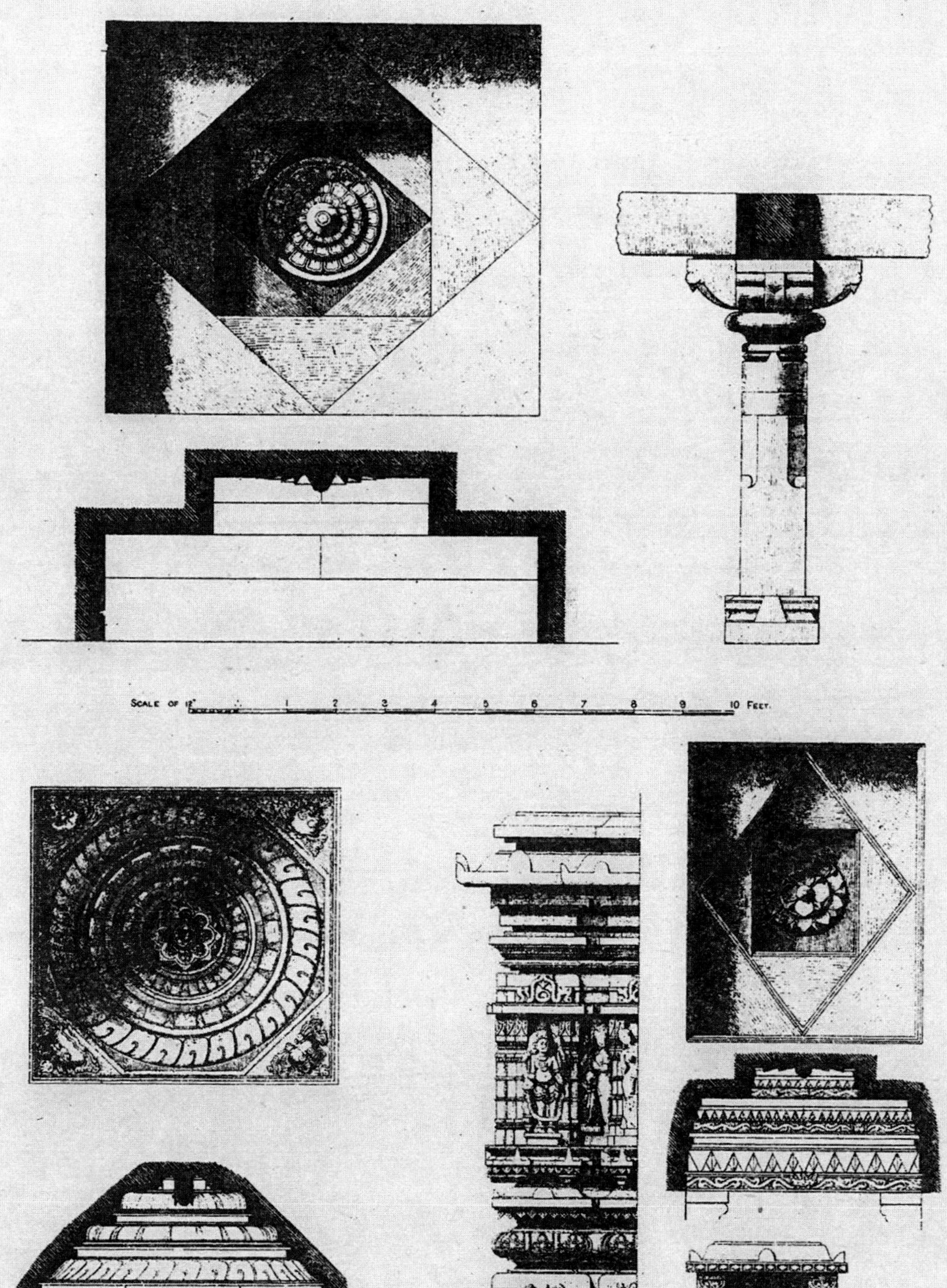

CEILING AND PILLAR FROM RAMESVARA, AND CEILING AND DETAILS FROM LAKSHMI-NARAYANA AT PEDGAON.

TEMPLE OF NAKTI AT KARJAT.

TEMPLE OF DEVI AT MANDAVG.

THE TEMPLE OF SIDDESVARA AT LIMPANGAON.

WOOD-CARVED HOUSE FRONT AT SRIGUNDA.

PLATE LXXXVII

PILLARS, SCREEN AND PLAN FROM SIDDHESVARA AT LIMPANGAON.

THE TEMPLE OF NAGANATHA AT KHATAV.

THE TEMPLE OF GANAPATI AT KHATAV.

PLATE LXXXIX

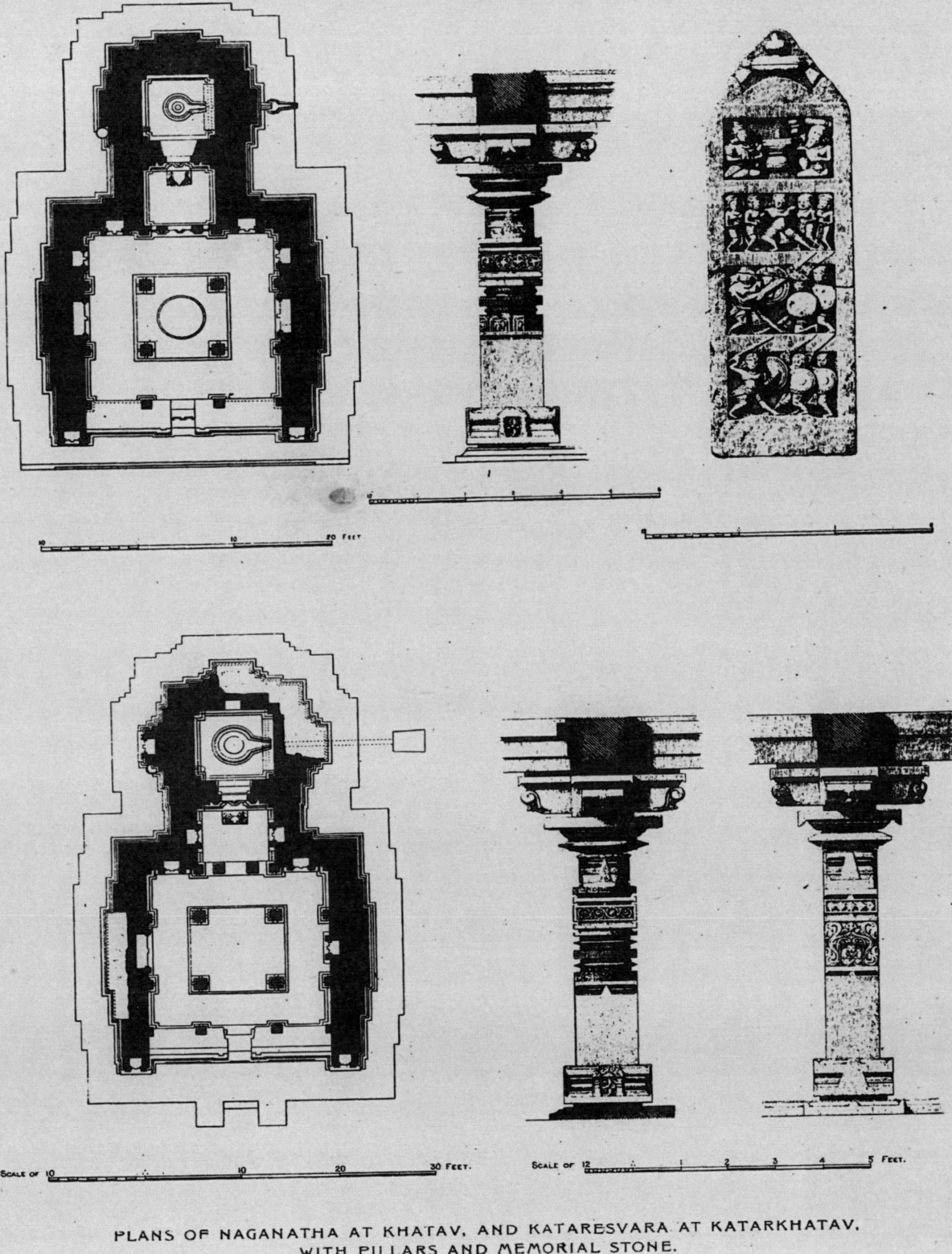


PLANS OF NAGANATHA AT KHATAV, AND KATARESVARA AT KATARKHATAV,
WITH PILLARS AND MEMORIAL STONE.

THE TEMPLE OF KATARESVARA AT KATARKHATAV.

THE TEMPLE OF RAMALINGA AT GURSALA.

PLATE XCI

TEMPLE OF SOMALINGA AT GURSALA.

TEMPLE OF SAMBHU-MAHADEVA AT SINGHANAPUR.

THE TEMPLE OF RAMALINGA AT GURSALA.

THE. TEMPLE OF AMRITESVARA AT SINGHANAPUR.

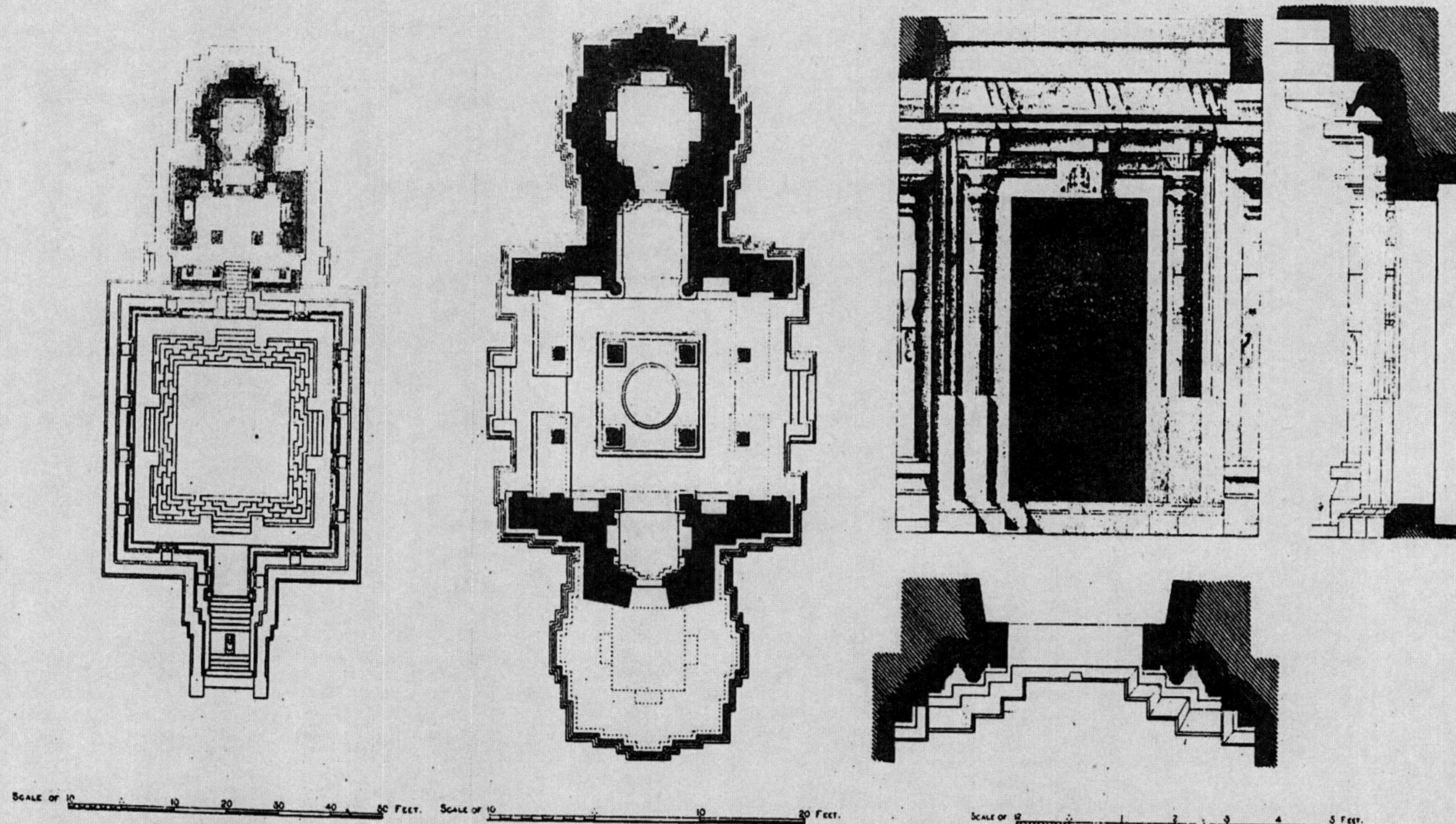


PLANS OF RAMALING AT GURSALA AND THE TEMPLE OF SIVA AT VELAPUR, WITH ELEVATION, SECTION AND PLAN OF DOORWAY.

PILLARS FROM THE OLD AND MODERN TEMPLES AT SINGHANAPUR.

TEMPLE OF SOMESVARA AT MALSIRAS.

TEMPLE ON THE TANK AT VELAPUR.

INTERIOR OF THE TEMPLE ON THE TANK AT VELAPUR.

MEMORIAL STONES AT VELAPUR.

MEMORIAL STONES FROM VELAPUR.

PLATE XCVIII

SCALE OF 12 — 2 FEET.

SCALE OF 12 — 1 FEET.

SCALE OF 12 — 2 FEET

SCALE OF 12 — 1 FEET.

IMAGES AND SCULPTURES FROM WARKUT AND VANGI.

PLATE XCIX

THE TEMPLE OF KALIKA DEVI AT BARSI-TAKLI.

PLATE C

THE BACK OF THE TEMPLE OF KALIKA DEVI AT BARSI-TAKLI.

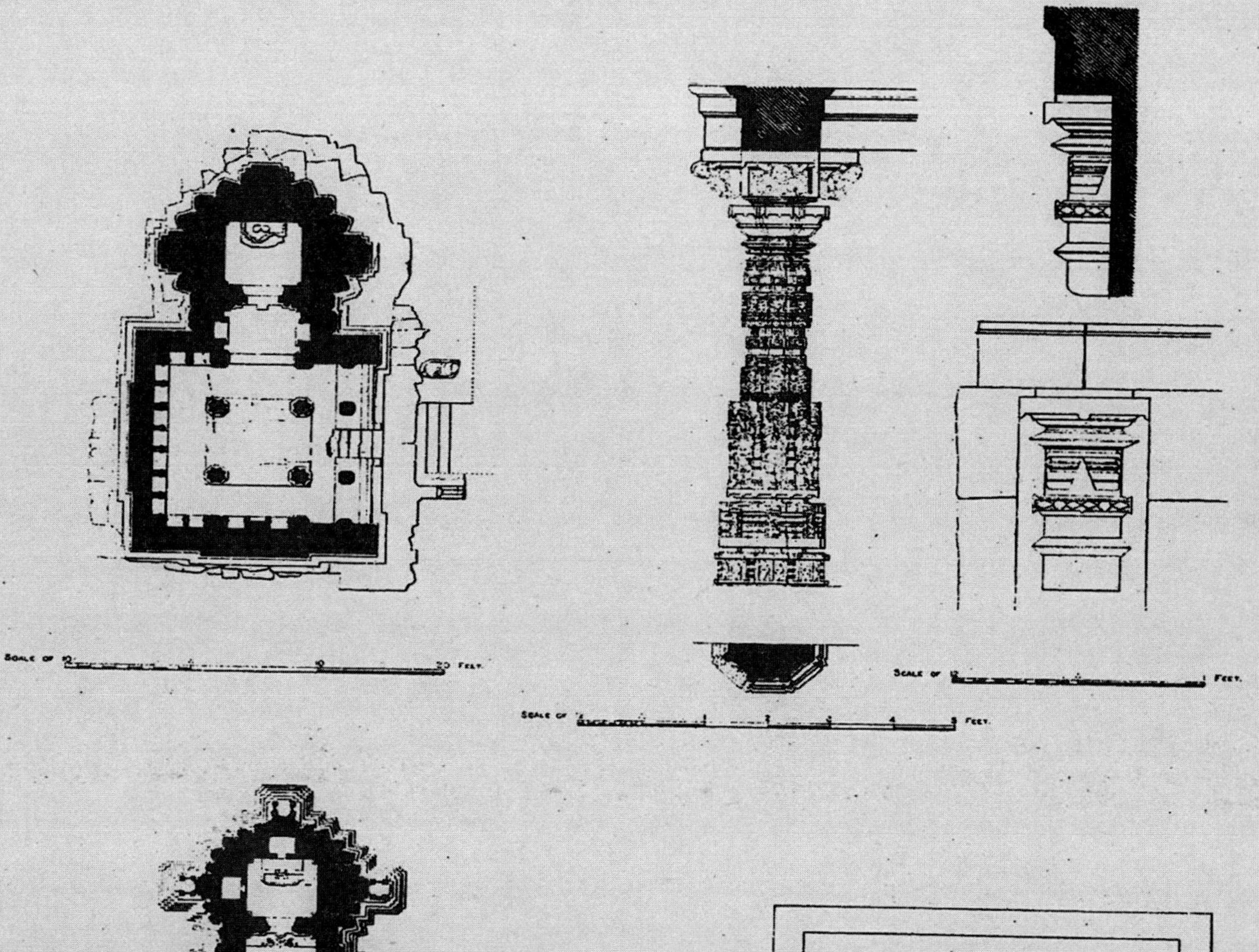

PLAN AND PILLAR OF THE TEMPLE OF KALIKA DEVI AT BARSI-TAKLI AND PLAN OF THE TEMPLE OF DAITYA SUDANA AT LONAR.

PLATE CII

THE TEMPLE OF ANTARIKSHA-PARSVANATHA AT SIRPUR.

DOORWAY OF ANTARIKSHA-PARSVANATHA AT SIRPUR.

THE TEMPLE OF DAITYA SUDANA AT LONAR.

THE OLD DHARAMASALA AT MEHKAR.

PLATE CIV

THE TEMPLE OF DAITYA SUDANA AT LONAR. FROM THE SOUTH-WEST.

PLATE CV

THE LAKE AND A TEMPLE AT LONAR.

TEMPLE AT BOTTOM OF DESCENT TO THE LAKE AT LONAR.

TEMPLE OUTSIDE THE WEST WALL OF THE VILLAGE AT SATGAON.

CEILING IN THE OLD TEMPLE AT SATGAON.

SIDE OF THE OLD TEMPLE AT SATGAON.

INTERIOR OF THE TEMPLE AT SATGAON.

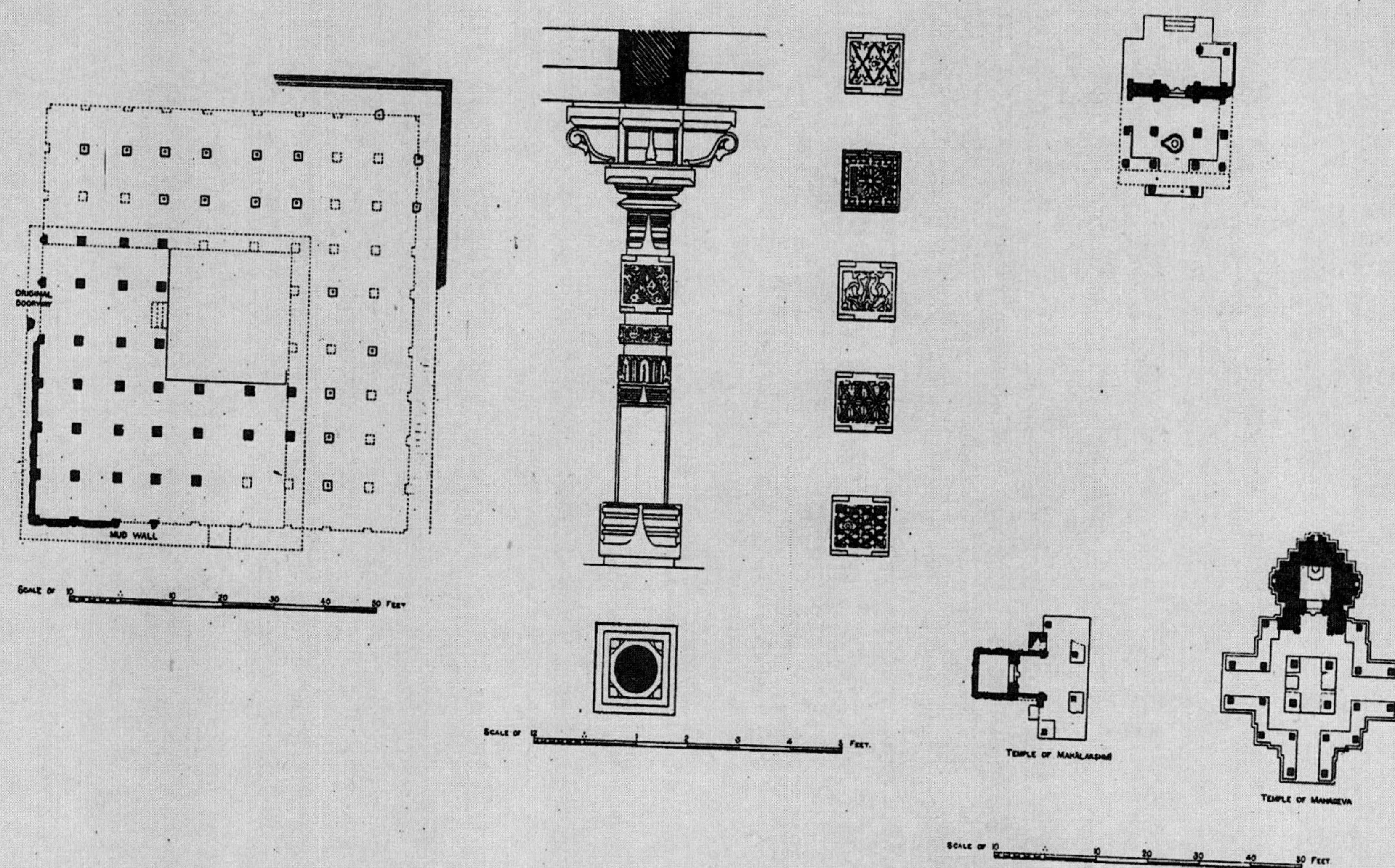


PLAN AND PILLAR OF THE OLD DHARMSALA AT MEHKAR, AND PLANS OF OLD TEMPLES AT SATGAON.

THE TEMPLE AT SAKEGAON FROM THE SOUTH-WEST.

THE TEMPLE AT SAKEGAON FROM THE SOUTH-EAST.

THREE-SHRINED TEMPLE AT KOTHALI.

DOORWAY OF THREE-SHRINED TEMPLE AT KOTHALI.

TEMPLE AT DHOTRA.

TEMPLE OF SUNDARA NARAYANA AT NASIK.

THE GREAT TEMPLE AT AUNDHA: THE FRONT.

THE GREAT TEMPLE AT AUNDHA: THE BACK

PLATE CXIV

A PORTION OF THE WALLS, AND THE FRONT ENTRANCE OF THE GREAT TEMPLE AT AUNDHA.

PILLARS OF THE PORCH, AND PILLARS INSIDE THE HALL OF THE GREAT TEMPLE AT AUNDHA.

*Published by*

**Facsimile Publisher**
Ashok Vihar, Delhi-110052 (India)
Website: www.facsimilepublisher.com

*Distributed by*

**Gyan Books Pvt. Ltd.**
5, Ansari Road, Daryaganj, New Delhi-110002 (India)
E-mail: books@gyanbooks.com, Website: www.gyanbooks.com

2 222000 012113